WALTER RAUSCHENBUSCH
AND HIS CONTRIBUTION
TO SOCIAL CHRISTIANITY

BY

ANNA M. SINGER, A. M.

Wipf & Stock
PUBLISHERS
Eugene, Oregon

Wipf and Stock Publishers
199 W 8th Ave, Suite 3
Eugene, OR 97401

Walter Rauschenbusch
and his contribution to Social Christianity
By Singer, Anna M.
ISBN 13: 978-1-55635-417-5
ISBN 10: 1-55635-417-7
Publication date 4/7/2007
Previously published by Gorham Press, 1926

TO

JOHN GODFREY HILL, PH. D.,
Professor of Biblical Literature,
University of Southern California,

GUSTAV A. BRIEGLEB, D. D.,
Pastor of Westlake Presbyterian Church,
Los Angeles, California, and

REVEREND B. JOHNSON REEMTSMA,
Pastor First Presbyterian Church,
Fowler, California,

who have given unstintedly of their time and
thought in making valuable criticisms.

FOREWORD

It was my great privilege to review the following pages when they were in manuscript form. The longer I read the more interesting and instructive they became. Going directly to the sources themselves, the author in her treatment of the life and work of Dr. Walter Rauschenbusch has gathered into one compact and convincing volume a broadminded survey of this great prophet of the new day. The work of the author deserves a hearty welcome on the part of the reading public as a well ordered, painstaking and valuable contribution to the subject in hand.

G. A. BRIEGLEB, D. D.
Pastor Westlake Presbyterian Church,
Los Angeles, California.

PREFACE

The subject of social Christianity and the possible application of Jesus' principles as a remedy for modern social problems appealed to the writer of this thesis while listening to the inspiring lectures of Doctor E. S. Bogardus, head of the Department of Sociology in the University of Southern California. Later, in the study of "Problems of Reconstruction", under the direction of Doctor R. D. Hunt, head of the Department of Economics, in the same institution, the interest in this particular subject deepened and grew until after further study, the writing of this book was the result.

The purpose of the study was to present a useful classification and review of Doctor Walter Rauschenbusch's Contribution to Social Christianity, since he firmly believed true religion and ethics to be inseparable in the solution of social problems.

Special thanks are due to Doctor Hunt, whose sympathy, encouragement and invaluable suggestions made the writing of this book possible.

For courtesies shown by other professors, by the City Librarian, and by Clarence A. Barbour, President of the Rochester Baptist Theological Seminary, for pamphlets and letters of information, the writer is specially indebted.

Acknowledgment is due also to Mrs. Mary Noble, Miss Katherine Foote and other friends in Los Angeles for helpful and sympathetic suggestions.

A. M. S.

CONTENTS

CHAPTER	PAGE
I. INTRODUCTION	13
1. Twentieth Century called, "Age of Social Questions"	15
2. Many Concerned about Social Problems Today	15
3. Walter Rauschenbusch, a Pioneer Prophet of Social Righteousness	15
II. A BRIEF SKETCH OF HIS LIFE	16
1. Parentage, Birth, Home and Early Life	16
2. Preparation for his Life-work	16
(a) Education	16
(b) Travels	17
3. Phases of his Professional Work	17
(a) Pastor in New York City	17
(b) Professorship at Rochester, New York	18
(1) Power as Teacher	19
(2) Influence on Students	19
(3) Personality	19
(c) Organizer and Lecturer	20
4. Author of Religious Books	21
III. A BRIEF CHARACTERIZATION OF HIS MAJOR BOOKS	22
1. Christianity and the Social Crisis	22
2. Prayers of the Social Awakening	23
3. Christianizing the Social Order	23
4. The Social Principles of Jesus	24
5. A Theology for the Social Gospel	24

His Teachings in Social Christianity

IV. 1. A HISTORICAL REVIEW OF THE CONCEPTIONS OF THE KINGDOM OF GOD TO THE PRESENT TIME	26
A. The Ideas of the Prophets	26
B. The Conception of John the Baptist	32
C. The Conception of Jesus' Followers and Others down to the Present Time	33

CHAPTER		PAGE
	2. The Teachings of Jesus Concerning the Kingdom of God	37
	A. His Teachings	37
	B. The Fundamental Social Principles of Jesus	42
V.	HIS TEACHINGS CONCERNING RACE PREJUDICE AND CLASS DISTINCTION	47
	1. All are Brothers in Christ	48
	2. Sense of Equality the Basis for Christian Morality	51
VI.	PERSONAL DISTRIBUTION OF WEALTH	53
	1. Wealth and its Pursuit	53
	(a) Some of the Dangers Connected with Accumulation of Wealth	54
	(b) The Moral Problem Concerning Property Ownership	58
	2. The Rich, the Poor, the Criminal and the Outcast	59
	(a) Jesus' Attitude Toward Each Class	59
	(b) The Personality of the most Wretched Being is Sacred	62
VII.	A REVIEW OF THE PRESENT SITUATION IN THE INDUSTRIAL WORLD	65
	1. Employer *versus* Employee	65
	Labor *versus* Wages	65
	Profit *versus* Life	65
	A. Employer *versus* Employee	66
	(1) Employer's Relation to Business Men	67
	(2) In Relation to His Employees	68
	(3) In Relation to the Consumer	70
	B. Labor *versus* Wages	72
	C. Profit *versus* Life	73
	(1) The Physical Fitness of the Laborer must be Protected	73
	(2) The Rise of the Working-class Involves an Increase in their Shares of the Profits	77

CHAPTER		PAGE
	2. Child Welfare and the Woman Movement	81
	(1) Child Welfare	81
	(a) The Child's Economic Value	82
	(b) The Rights of a Child	83
	(c) Child-labor	85
	(2) The Woman Movement	86
	(a) The Factory Woman	87
	(b) Some Moral Aspects of "The Woman Movement"	88
	(c) The Rise of Women and their Increased Responsibilities	91
VIII.	MILITARISM, WAR AND CONFLICT WITH EVIL	93
	1. Cause of World War	94
	2. Problem of International Peace	95
	3. Militarism and the Danger of the Militant Spirit	96
	4. Conflict with Evil	99
IX.	THE CHURCH AS A SOCIAL FACTOR OF SALVATION	102
	1. Its Influence in the Past	102
	2. Its Faults and Mistakes in the Past	108
	3. Its Present Opportunity	113
X.	CONCLUSION	122
	1. Essence of His Contribution	122
	2. Criticisms and Comments	127
	3. An Estimate of His Influence	130

WALTER RAUSCHENBUSCH
AND HIS CONTRIBUTION TO SOCIAL CHRISTIANITY

Chapter I

INTRODUCTION

All through the long centuries of history, men have struggled against tyranny and oppression, and have suffered and died for some new realization of Liberty and Justice. Mankind has recently passed through another crucifixion; ten million soldiers died on the battle-fields of Europe; ten million civilians suffered indirectly, because of the War.

But the Supreme Moral and Social Task of every man and woman now is, to live and labor for the full fruition of democracy as faithfully and heroically, as did those who died to "Make the World safe for Democracy."

There never was in all history such a call for true patriots. If ever a man loved his country and his kind, now is the time to demonstrate it. Quoting from J. Stitt Wilson: "The gathering clouds of world-tragedy, call every true man and woman in America to the most selfless devotion to Christian Democracy."[1]

Civilization only began with the keeping of historic records, with man's coming to social self-consciousness and with his beginning of the control and conquest of the mental or spiritual element in his life. Then came years of mastery over physical nature and human nature, and so on through, the transition from lower to higher stages

[1] Wilson, J. Stitt, *Constructive Christian Democracy*. Address delivered at the University of Southern California, April, 1919.

of civilization is intermediated by pattern ideas or ideals. This principle applies to the great changes in religion and morals.

Christianity is a new set of pattern ideas marking the dawn of a new civilization with non predatory morality on a humanitarian basis.

Jesus initiated the revolution in religious and moral ideas for which the whole of human history had been preparing.

In him we find the supreme development of the idea that to serve God was through service to men, no matter what their condition, occupation or nationality might be. Today the world needs this same understanding of the social significance of Christianity.

In these times the humanitarianism of Christianity must become more pronounced. The spirit of Constructive Christian Democracy with this passion for Social Justice and Economic Righteousness, perceives "the unutterable sacredness of souls; respects and reverences the bottom mud-sill of the human race; and demands for each and all, the full measures of social, political and industrial advantage for complete human living."[2]

Today the race is coming to social self-consciousness, and men are discovering that they are social beings. Men are learning that our personal life is rooted in the life of humanity and that it flourishes in that soil, deriving its richest nourishment from it and living because others live.

The transformation of our whole economic life, from the basis of mad competition and strife for profits, to the basis of co-operation and mutual service to humanity, involves an endless chain of social questions to be settled during the present era.

Since every age is, in a sense, peculiar, this age also has problems that are distinctive. It has been said by a promi-

[2]Wilson, J. Stitt, *Constructive Christian Democracy.* 3.

nent European Philosopher, that the twentieth century will be called by succeeding generations, "The Age of Social Questions." Whether this be true or not, for the solution of these problems, there rests upon the Church, upon educators, and upon every Christian citizen, a much larger responsibility than most of them have as yet begun to understand. However, never in human history were there so many people, learned and ignorant, employers and employed, rich and poor, so seriously concerned about the question of social justice, the problem of economic righteousness and the realizing of social dreams. At every turn, man is confronted with a problem, in the solution of which, he is told the whole world is interested.

It would be a serious mistake to say that the present day is without its real prophets, or that their voices are not heard above the turmoil and confusion.

As such a prophet of social righteousness, the late Walter Rauschenbusch stood in the very front rank of the men of our day. President Clarence Barbour of the Rochester Theological Seminary, says that he was a pioneer in this great and until recently, untouched field. By Graham Taylor he was considered the "foremost interpreter of contemporary social Christianity."

While much has been accomplished by present day social activities throughout the world, many of the social programs are without Christianity. The needs are too deep for surface remedies and Doctor Rauschenbusch recognizing this fact, places all of his social welfare principles and propositions firmly on the basis of practical social Christianity as taught by Jesus himself.

Great men need not our praise, yet by a brief sketch of his life, and a condensed review of his works, we wish to call attention to one who made a distinct contribution to his generation, and who has left a deposit of influence in the current of human history.

CHAPTER II

A BRIEF SKETCH OF HIS LIFE.

Augustus Rauschenbusch, one of the grand old men of the Church, came from Germany to this country, with those who sought freedom of thought and speech during the period of unrest which prevailed in that land preceding and following the revolution of 1848.

In 1851 he spent four months in the county of Waterloo, Ontario, Canada, where there were many people of his nationality. Among these he labored, and preached the gospel, baptizing many and laying the foundation of several churches.

Having a keen and deep intellect, animated with a glowing religious spirit, he was a scholar with interesting eccentricities.

He voted for Freemont and Lincoln for the Presidency, before Walter was born.

This son Walter was an American by birth, and first saw the light of day in Rochester, New York, on October 4th. 1861, where he was reared and received his early education. Having spent most of his life in this city, many of his choicest friendships were with Rochester folks; and having always taken an active interest in the affairs of this place, it became dear to him above all others.

Although he was called a "Rochester product," he received his preparatory education abroad; graduating with first honors from the Classical Gymnasium in Guetersloh, Germany, in 1883.

In 1884, he received his A. B. degree from the University of Rochester, and in 1886 he graduated from the Rochester Theological Seminary, where he was ordained as a Baptist minister.

It was not surprising that Rauschenbusch chose the

ministry for his profession, for upon him fell a family heritage handed down by a long line of university trained ministerial ancestors and kinsmen.¹

From 1886 to 1897 he was pastor of the little Second German Baptist Church in the city of New York, impelled to accept that position by his willingness for sacrificial service and his love for the poor.

In 1891-92 he again studied abroad, as also in 1907 and 1908.²

While pastor in New York, he secured a very able assistant, in the person of Miss Pauline Rother of Milwaukee, whom he married in 1893.³ To her, his children and his entire family circle, he gave himself with constancy, tenderness and sacrificial devotion throughout the remainder of his life.

For eleven years he spent himself without measure working among German Immigrants and tenement house dwellers of New York.

During his ministry in that city, through premature exposure after a severe illness, there came to him the affliction which was to remain with him to the end. Henceforth the world of sound was largely closed to him. Those who knew him most intimately, know best how keenly he realized the handicap; yet with a smile, he always bore his deprivation splendidly, and did not allow it to interfere with that gracious, sparkling humor of his, which was so marked a characteristic of his thinking and of his word.⁴

He was "shepherd of the poor, insignificant and oppressed of every race; friend, unfailing in humor, in wisdom, and in suggestion."⁵

¹Taylor, Graham, Obituary of Walter Rauschenbusch. *Survey.* XL, 498.
²*The International Encyclopedia.* XIX, 569-70.
³*Who's Who in America,* X, 1918-1919.
⁴Moehlman, Prof. Conrad H. *Memorial Address.* November 18, 1918.
⁵*Ibid.*

His sympathies were with those whom birth, circumstances and conditions had thrown under the wheels of misfortune. He loved all people, especially those who bore the burden and heat of the day. No man lives whose heart ever went out more tenderly toward those who are bearing the unequal burdens of human life. What he saw of actual conditions, developed his innately democratic spirit and made him the champion of true democracy, of the brotherhood of man, and of the cooperative commonwealth.

After serving eleven years as pastor in New York city, Rauschenbusch returned to Rochester in 1897, where he remained for twenty-one years as Professor in the Rochester Theological Seminary; teaching New Testament from 1897 to 1902, and Church History from 1902 to 1918. In the field of Church history he was without a peer. He made that history live and throb with meaning. Successive classes of students recognized their debt to him, because he was illuminating, thought-compelling, and inspiring.

To him, the history of the Church was always considered in the relation to the living God, whose footsteps are everywhere found in the story of the nations and of the Church, for him who has eyes to see. He loved the Church and among all other institutions, held her incomparable.

He was fortunate in possessing so many friends who understood him.

"When flattering and attractive invitations came from the distant West or nearer East—calls that would have moved the ordinary mortal to a new love—Professor Rauschenbusch only the more resolutely determined to give himself without stint to Rochester."[6]

Being a wonderful teacher, within the field which he

The Record, The Rochester Seminary Bulletin, November, 1918, p. 18.

A Brief Sketch of His Life

chose to develop, he moved as master. His teaching was luminous; the abstract became concrete and real with him, and clear-cut to the minds of those whom he taught.

As he saw the unfolding of great principles, so he saw the steady advance of the ever-manifesting purposes of God, through the ages and about the circle of the globe.

In his professional work he was a magnet for students. Many men who came to the Seminary, felt the lure of his presence and were attracted there because he was one of the instructors. Many of them deliberately chose humble and hard fields of work, because of his personal inspiration, and all of his students came to feel the power of his message. They were inspired by his challenge to undertake tasks requiring sacrifice and courage.

In his description of the personality of Water Rauschenbusch, Ray Stannard Baker tells us that he was a tall, spare man, with a humorous twinkle in his eyes. He possessed a special appreciation of the humorous and drove home to the minds of the students, many a plain truth, by stressing the ridiculous side of some situation.[1]

Though much occupied with his studies and his classes, yet he found time for active interest in the affairs of his city and neighborhood; his spare moments he occupied at a working bench with a set of carving tools.

Many a class-room embarrassment has been saved by the Professor's humor, but his humor was never needed to save the situation; it served the higher end of illuminating the exposition of his theme. He developed his humor through the actual situations which the personages of history created.

Unlike many other scholars, he never avoided warm, human contact with those about him.

His deafness confined him largely to the lecture method in his teaching, yet he povided an occasional quiz, at

[1] Baker, Ray Stannard. Personality of Walter Rauschenbusch. *American Magazine*, December, 1910, p. 18.

which time he heard through the ears of a member of the class who served as reporter.

It was a perpetual surprise and mystery to the class, that an instructor so handicapped, and reading only scrappy longhand notes, could diagnose so accurately the exact degree of their ignorance of the topic under discussion.[8]

Because of his deafness he seemed to live in a world of deep thought and meditation, concerning those things which are nearest to the heart of God, and most needful to man.

Doctor Rauschenbusch was a great lover of nature, enjoying picnic suppers, camping, canoeing, swimming and fishing. When in company with others, there never was anything perfunctory in his interest.

During vacations, he and his family were supremely happy in their summer home on Sturgeon Lake, where he enjoyed the simple, pure, elevating pleasures which nature offers. His sympathy and appreciation of life was as broad as humanity, and his hospitality was unusual.

It was his custom to take the different members of the student body home with him for a noon-day meal, thus giving opportunity for close fellowship in his study and about the family table.

During his faithful attention to his duties in the Seminary, Dr. Rauschenbusch constantly responded to the calls for service beyond the Seminary walls, though he could not respond affirmatively to a tenth of the insistent demands for his message. Besides, his great abilities and services were increasingly recognized outside of Rochester, for there were country-wide demands for his lecturing and for his writings, which for years, had far transcended his ability to meet.[9]

[8]Robins, Professor Henry, *The Record*. November, 1918, p. 82.
[9]Taylor, Graham, Obituary of Walter Rauschenbusch. *Survey*, XL, 493.

Not only did Dr. Rauschenbusch touch and help to mould great multitudes of men, but he helped to mould institutions as well. For many years he was secretary of the Baptist Congress, co-founder of the 'Brotherhood Kingdom' and a faithful worker in the Young Men's Christian Association. He was translator of hymns into many tongues; hymns that have circled the globe and will continue in their work of ministry long after the day when the voice of their writer was stilled.

He was also a poet, so modest that even the circle of his friends remained unaware of his genius. Besides having gifts as poetic artist, he was also an able essayist, contributor to the daily press and monthly magazine, editor of religious periodicals and author of many published books, being called "home" with several others under contemplation.

Through the printed page, this great teacher ministered to the needs of unnumbered thousands of hungry spirits. Even during the last days of his illness, he dictated a paper for Home Mission Society workers.

His death occured July 25, 1918, the immediate cause of which was a surgical operation. His nearest friends believe that his grief over the condition of the world was a contributing cause. The World War had been shattering for years the ideals of human brotherhood, for which he had so steadfastly labored, and it was thought that his grief had greatly depleted his powers, so that he did not have his full vitality for recuperation.

He was an ideal husband, father, teacher, pastor and friend. In his death, the whole church loses one of its most fearless thinkers; the Christian social movement, one of its most widely recognized and deeply beloved leaders, and the inter-national social democracy, a living link connecting its economic ideals with those spiritual resources upon which their realization depends.[10]

[10]Taylor, Graham, Walter Rauschenbusch, *Survey*, XL, 498.

Chapter III

A BRIEF CHARACTERIZATION OF
HIS MAJOR BOOKS

1—*"Christianity And The Social Crisis"* is the first book of Walter Rauschenbusch's major works, published in 1907. It is the book which is said to have had more influence in remaking the spirit of the Church to meet modern demands, than any other book of recent years.

Its argument is strongly based on economic, historical, ethical and religious grounds; its temper and tone are admirably dispassionate and judicial.

During his ministry in New York among the working people, Professor Rauschenbusch's social education began, and the connection between religious and social questions, was revealed to him. This revelation led him to revise his whole study of the Bible which resulted in the writing of this book.

It was his testimony to the religious life of the nation; and its wide influence is in a measure due to the fact that it came just when the social awakening of the country was evident, and when thousands of people needed an expression for the new religious and humanitarian ideas which were coming to them.

In this book he discusses the historical roots of Christianity, the social aims of Jesus, the present crisis and the stake of the Church in the social movement.

2—Professor Rauschenbusch distinctly recognized the subjective value of prayer and made effective use of it. He also believed in the objective influence of social prayer. To hear him pray, was to feel a benediction. Prayer not only revived his spirit, but seemed to bring renewal to all his powers. It was the custom of this teacher to open his class lectures by a brief prayer to his Heavenly Father; consequently it was no surprise to the students and his friends when, in 1910, he published his second major book, a volume of *"Prayers of the Social Awakening."*

This little book consists of short, definite, expressive petitions for people in almost every walk of life or circumstance.[1]

Like his messages, these prayers are free from those platitudes and stilted phrases which too often characterize prayer. They reveal the heart of the author, uncovering his imperishable treasure, as well as his sincere yearnings for humanity. Each in itself expresses clearly, directly or indirectly, his views and hopes pertaining to the prominent problems of social injustice and unrighteousness. It has been said that no man since the Church began, has done more to set Christendom praying on social problems.[2]

3—The third book of his major works is, *"Christianizing the Social Order,"* published in 1912. It is an impressive sequel to his first suggestive and stimulating volume.[3] In some ways it is an answer to the challenge raised by the first book. Having advocated in it a regeneration of the moral order, he had to meet the demand, "How shall it be done?"

In this book he describes the social awakening of religious organizations, seeks to show that the Christianizing of the social order, was the original aim of Christianity; he analyzes what is, and what is not Christian, in our social order, discusses the direction of progress and the method of advance.

"There is no more stirring plea in our literature for

[1]Several of these prayers and others similar in thought, were published from time to time, in the *American Magazine,* during 1910.
[2]*The Record,* The Rochester Theological Seminary Bulletin, November, 1918, p. 50.
[3]*The Record,* The Rochester Theological Seminary Bulletin, November, 1918.

renovation of our social system, than Professor Rauschenbusch's appeal in this book. It is unequivocal, but after all it is not radical.[4]

4—The fourth of his major works, is a book on the "*Social Principles of Jesus.*" Proceeding by the inductive method, it re-interprets familiar passages of the Gospel, so that one can never forget them. This 'literary Jewel' of Professor Rauschenbusch's is arranged in text-book form, with many searching questions in each daily assignment, which are left unanswered in the book.

His clear-cut comments formulate in simple propositions the fundamental convictions of Jesus about the social and ethical relations and duties of men.

There are a thousand sermons in it; hundreds of colleges and university groups have used it in their courses, and during the world-war a thousand soldiers studied it.[5]

It reveals the reality and intensity of Jesus' convictions regarding social life, and indicates with great force, his solution of social difficulties.[6]

5—His fifth book, "*A Theology for the Social Gospel,*" is primarily a book for ministers, whose eyes have watched for the dawn of that day of liberation. But the book is for others too—for all who are profoundly dissatisfied with present creeds and catechisms and who are passionately anxious that the vital teachings of the Galilean shall find expression in these troubled times.

It is a strong work, based on sound learning and inspired with prophetic spirit. While Professor Rauschenbusch was not a doctrinal theologian, he felt that the necessity of approaching systematic theology from the outside might be of real advantage.

[4]Small, A. W., *American Journal of Sociology*, XVIII, 809.
[5]*The Record*, The Rochester Theological Seminary Bulletin, November, 1918, p. 48.
[6]*Ibid.*

The main proposition of this book, is an attempt to furnish a systematic theology large enough and vital enough, to match and back the social gospel.[7]

It is a book that is perceptive of the truth in *old* systems and insistent on the necessity and value of the *new* order of ideas.[8]

In it, he has carried the foundations of his social program and philosophy, deeper than ever. At the same time, the book has a rare charm of style, and reveals the unusual ability of the author to vitalize old forms of thought.

In it he also shows that "a re-adjustment and expansion of theology is necessary, feasible, desirable and legitimate"[9] so that it will form an adequate basis for the social gospel.

[7] Rauschenbusch, *A Theology for the Social Gospel*, p. 1.
[8] *The Record*, The Rochester Theological Seminary Bulletin, November, 1918, p. 47.
[9] *Ibid.*

CHAPTER IV

HISTORICAL REVIEW OF THE CONCEPTIONS OF THE KINGDOM OF GOD

I

A The Ideas of the Prophets

The social background, spirit, and message of Doctor Rauschenbusch as found in practically all of his major works, is the one great fundamental truth that the "Kingdom of God," as expounded by the prophets and Jesus, means the salvation of the social order; that in the purposes of God, the 'Kingdom' is not only a hope for the future but that it is already existent here on earth, and that the supreme task of every Christian citizen, is to co-operate with God in the fulfillment of this, the greatest of all social duties.

In this chapter, it is the aim merely to *point out* the various conceptions and teachings of the Hebrew prophets and others, concerning the Kingdom as Doctor Rauschenbusch reviews them.

Since the prophets are the beating hearts of the Old Testament, a brief study of their social influence in the history of social movements is indispensable for any true comprehension of the mind of Jesus, because with them he linked his points of view. Also, in so far as men have caught the true spirit of these prophets, the influence of the Old Testament has been one of the great permanent forces making for democracy and social justice, in our time as in theirs.

(1) In the primitive life of the Israelitish tribes, the religion of the common folk was based on the belief that Jehovah was the tribal god of Israel.

The essential thing in their religion was, not morality, but the ceremonial method of placating the god, securing his gifts and ascertaining his wishes.

There were certain forms of moral evil which he hated, and certain duties which he loved and blessed, but the surest way of remaining in his favor was to sacrifice, duly and plentifully.

But the actual life of the nation, especially of its ruling classes, never 'squared' with the religious ideals, and to the prophets, the injustice and oppression around them seemed intolerable. They ardently hoped for a day, and expected its coming, when things would be as they ought to be.

(2) This great day would inaugurate a new age, the Kingdom of God. The Jewish people believed the Kingdom to mean the Reign of God over the children of Israel; but the prophets, whatever their ideas concerning the Kingdom were, believed that all the *world* was God's field, and that the King wanted a right life in his subjects, and the righting of social wrongs.

(3) Isaiah therefore cried out in warning: "Your hands are full of blood! Cease to do evil! Learn to do right! Seek justice! Relieve the oppressed! Secure justice for the orphaned and plead for the widow!"

Again, Isaiah urged the abolition of social oppression and injustice, as the only way of regaining God's favor for the Jewish nation. If they would vindicate the cause of the helpless and oppressed, then he would freely pardon. On the one hand, he promised them economic prosperity, and on the other, he threatened continual war. "If ye be willing and obedient, ye shall eat the food of the land; but if ye refuse and rebel, ye shall be devoured with the sword."[1]

(4) Micah pointed out the uselessness of sacrifice to

[1] *Christianity and the Social Crisis*, 5-6, Isaiah 1: 10-17.

God without doing justly, without loving kindness, and walking humbly before God.[2]

(5) Amos and Jeremiah tried to teach that obedience was all that God had required.[3,4]

The early prophets, even the most aristocratic among them, were the champions of the poor. In Jeremiah and in the prophetic Psalms, the "poor" as a class, are made identical with the "meek" and "godly", and the "rich" and "wicked" are almost synonymous terms.[5]

"Since Amos, it was the Alpha and Omega of prophetic preaching to insist on right and justice, to warn against the oppression of the poor and helpless."[6]

(6) The prophets demanded right moral conduct as the sole test and fruit of religion, but the morality which they had in mind was not the private morality of pious, detached souls, but the social morality of the nation.

They foretold future events on the basis of the conviction that God rules with righteousness. This they preached, and backed up their preaching with vigilant participation in public activity and discussion.

The belief in a future life and future reward and punishment, was almost absent in Hebrew religion. To live to an honored old age, to see his children and children's children, to enjoy the fruit of his labor in peace, under his own vine and fig-tree; that was all the heaven to which the pious Israelite looked forward. The land belonged to Jehovah the national God, and God must prove his justice here or never. The popular feeling was that God would stand by them, and they expected their God to act on the maxim, "My country right or wrong."

The prophets denied this. They thought that the relation of the nation to Jehovah rested on moral condi-

---

[2] *Micah* 6: 6-8.
[3] *Amos* 5: 25. [4] *Jeremiah* 7: 22-23.
[5] *Ibid* (1) 13.
[6] *Ibid* 11.

tions. They repudiated the idea of favoritism in the divine government. God moves on the plane of universal and impartial ethical law. Their religion and its teachings became inter-national in its horizon and more profoundly ethical in its nature. Furthermore, they were heralds of the fundamental truth that religion and ethics are inseparable, and that ethical conduct is the supreme and sufficient religious act; "which principle, if it had been fully adopted in our religious life, would have turned the full force of the religious impulse, into the creation of right moral conduct and would have made the unchecked growth and accumulation of injustice impossible."[7]

The prophets were public men, whose interests were in public affairs and in the domain of public affairs, politics were to be controlled in the name of God. They launched the condemnation of Jehovah against injustice and oppression and taught that God rules justly in the affairs of governments and nations and only what is just shall endure.

Later, in the history of the Hebrew nation, when the national life itself was destroyed by the foreign conquerors, the Jewish nation as such, was blotted out; the religious history and the ceremonial worship of Israel, were the only bond of national unity that survived.

(7) The prophet Jeremiah began the turn toward individual piety. It is assumed that he and those who followed him, now set themselves deliberately to build a new religious community of regenerate souls. They turned their backs on the Jewish nation, and created the Jewish church. They insisted on personal holiness, not because that was the end of all religion, but because it was the condition and guarantee of national restoration. Thus, the idea of the Kingdom of God became entirely

[7]*Christianity and the Social Crisis,* 7-8.

changed, resulting in a separation between the political and religious interests. However, it is a mistake to assume that the Kingdom of God meant the same thing to all the prophets, even at that time.

(8) Ezekiel who lived during the Exile, also cherished the national hope; but while the older prophets had condemned the sins of man against man, especially injustice and oppression, Ezekiel dwelt on the sins of man against God. Not justice, but holiness became the fundamental requirement. Religion became more priestly and ritual, with a timid and legal reverence for externals.

"When the life of the nation withered away under the mailed fist of an alien power, and the attainment of future improvements was torn from its control, the character of the national hope underwent another continual and gradual change. By contact with foreign religious life during the Exile, the belief in a great organized Kingdom of Evil, had become a vital part of Jewish thought."

"It is profoundly pathetic to see how a people, paralyzed, broken on the rack and almost destroyed, still clung to its national existence and believed in its political future."[8]

While the ideal of the Kingdom of God was a social possession of the nation, it rose and declined with the outward condition and the inner spirit of the whole people. "When the nation lost its independence, its home, its neighborhood life and social coherence in the great Exile, its national hope gained in passion but lost in sanity."[9]

"Before the Exile, the prophets stood with both feet on the realities of national life. They expected the reign of God to come by an act of Jehovah and to connect with the present conditions and grow out of them, but during the Exile all their optimism was projected far into the

[8] *Christianity and the Social Crisis*, 85.
[9] *Christianizing the Social Order*, 58.

future."[10] Sitting in enforced helplessness, history seemed to them like a predetermined scheme.

(9) "After the coming in contact with the great Babylonian and Persian monarchies, and the Persian religion, a still more decisive change came about."[11]

Their horizon was widened and the national judgment enlarged into a world judgment; the national salvation into a cosmic renewal; the Messiah of the Davidic line into a heavenly deliverer. It was no longer a plain human fight against physical adversaries, but a supernal contest against spiritual principalities and powers, and the demoniac forces would have to be overthrown if the Kingdom of God was to be set up.

To the Jews, the Kingdom of God meant the triumph of Judaism, and all the kings of the world would have become tributary to the Jewish empire.

Within a short time before the arrival of Jesus, the universal expectation was that the Messiah would hoist the flag of revolt, and slay the oppressors, either by the breath of his mouth or by the sword of the faithful. Then the capital of the world would be shifted from Rome to Jerusalem.

The idea of the Kingdom was filled with democratic spirit, but it had come down from despotic times and was cast in monarchical forms. The Messiah was to rule as a King, and his followers were to rule as his courtiers.

(10) At that time, to all devout Jews, the Mosaic law and the Rabbinic law were the core of their religion, much as the Church is, to many pious Catholics today. Consequently the Kingdom of God did not mean the abolition of the Law, but its enthronement. It was this hope of the Kingdom that made the Pharisee so punctilious and rigid.

To the great mass of men then and now, material plenty

[10] *Ibid.*
[11] *Ibid,* 54.

and comfort were the real substance of any good time coming. Religious obedience was the price they must pay to get on the inside. Economic wealth was the end; morality and religion, the means. The popular expectation was, that the Messianic revolution was to happen with magic suddenness.

B The Conception of John the Baptist

The Christian movement began with John the Baptist. "The Law and the prophets were until John; from that time the Gospel of the Kingdom of God is preached and every man entereth violently into it."[12]

(1) "The subtance of John's message was the same old prophetic demand for ethical obedience."[13] He himself, accepted Jesus as the one who was to continue and consummate his own work.

Both Jesus and the people felt generally, that in John they had an incarnation of the spirit of the ancient prophets. He wore their austere garb; he shared their utter fearlessness, their ringing speech, their consciousness of speaking an inward message of God. He spoke only of repentance and of ceasing from wrong-doing. He demolished the self-confidence of the Jew, and his pride of descent and religious monopoly, just as Amos and Jeremiah had done.

(2) Now was the time to repent and by the badge of baptism to enroll with the purified remnant.[14]

(3) The way to prepare for the Messianic era was to institute a brotherly life, and to equalize social inequalities; to stop being parasites and to live on their honest earnings.[15]

[12] *Matthew* 11: 2-19, *Luke* 7: 18-35.
[13] *Christianity and the Social Crisis*, 49.
[14] *Matthew* 3: 5-12.
[15] *Luke* 3: 10-14.

J̦ohn would not have been so silent about the ordinary requirements of piety and so intensely emphatic in demanding the abolition of social wrongs, if he had not felt that here were the real obstacles to the coming of the Kingdom of God.

He put the Kingdom on an ethical basis, but it was still the social hope and it required social morality.

According to our Evangelists, the work of John, who was the fore-runner of Jesus, came to an end, because he had attacked Herod Antipas for his marriage with Herodias.[16]

C The Conceptions of Jesus' Followers and Others to the Present Time

Jesus accepted John as his fore-runner and after his baptism the power of his own mission was upon him. "If the followers of Jesus had preserved his thought and spirit without leakage, evaporation, or adulteration, it would be a unique fact in history."[17] "But they did not; even his early disciples did not have the same all-embracing and lofty conceptions of the Kingdom of God."[18]

(1) The Church early developed Christian Sacraments and superstitious rites which were to be used to placate and appease the Father of Jesus.

The main current of this Christian life, finally resulted in Catholic Christianity, followed other channels and left Jewish Christianity entirely isolated.

Whatever the other new ideas of the Kingdom dwindled into, the hope of the immediate return of Christ dominated the life of primitive Christianity, and this return of the Lord meant the inauguration of the Kingdom of God.

[16]*Matthew* 14: 3-5.
[17]*Christianity and the Social Crisis*, 94.
[18]*Ibid.*

However, the early Christians were no more unanimous about their eschatology than the Jews had been.

(2) Paul expected an immediate spiritualization of the entire Cosmos. The dead would be raised in a spiritual body: the living would be transformed into the same kind of body; for flesh and blood in the nature of things could not share in that spiritual Kingdom. Death would cease, nature would be glorified, and the children of God would be manifested in their glory. His entire outlook was almost devoid of social elements and to him the spirit was all. This material world could only be saved by ceasing to exist.[19]

(3) Other early Christians held that the material world, of course would end some day, but first there would be a really good life on earth. When Satan and his hosts were chained and imprisoned, and Christ and his saints reigned instead; then injustice and oppression would cease at last. This is the type of Christian hope expressed in the Apocalypse of St. John.

"At the end of a thousand years there would be a last rallying of the powers of evil, a final spasm of judgment, and then this earth would pass away."[20] The new earth which he mentions is only a glorified old earth with a shining city, and ever-bearing fruit trees, and a crystal river and nations that pass in and out through its gates.

(4) This idea was opposed by the Greek Church fathers, who could not admit a glorification of the material world in millennial splendor. Then when the Empire accepted Christianity as the State religion, the millennial hope was practically abandoned by the leaders of the Church, while the common people long clung to it.

In the Greek world of the first Christian centuries, the longing for eternal life was exceedingly strong, and the hope for any collective salvation almost non-existent.

[19]*Christianity and the Social Crisis*, 105.
[20]*Ibid*, 105-106.

"Baptism sterilized the leaven of sin and implanted eternal life."[21] Confirmation conveyed the Holy Ghost; extreme unction prepared the dying soul; masses and indulgences followed the soul even across the chasm of death to shorten the stay in purgatory and hasten the entrance into heaven.

(5) While this 'other worldly' longing was Greek in its origin, the reformatory sects of the Middle Ages shared it with them and with the Roman Catholic Church.

(6) Even in devout Protestantism, a deep longing for heaven, and distrust of the body as an enemy of the soul were regarded as marks of a Christian frame of mind.

The main aim set before Christians was to save their souls from eternal woe, to have communion with God now and hereafter and live God-fearing lives. It was an individualistic religion concentrated on the future life.

The desire for rest in heaven is not the social hope of the Reign of God on earth, with which Christianity set out. 'Other-worldly' religion developed only those ideas and those ethical motives in religion which served the salvation of the individual in the life to come.

Even the immortal works of Dante, Milton and Bunyan prove how completely even the greatest minds of that age lived in the spiritual world; and in the generation just preceding ours, this 'other-wordly' concentration of religious desires and energy still dominated the Christian life.

It practically constitutes the Gospel as preached today. The really effective religious ideas are more faithfully mirrored by the hymns of a given time than by its theology and sermons, and a study of our hymnals, gives an overwhelming impression of the predominance of otherworldly desires. This type of religion makes the eternal choice between right and wrong concrete, and it

[21]*Christianizing the Social Order*, 74.

strengthens the dawning consciousness of God and the higher life, in the young. Strong faith in a life to come has been one of the most powerful forces of social control in the past, a chief influence in making the present life clean, tender and worth living."

But after all, the atmosphere of the longing for death and detachment from this world, is not the atmosphere in which Jesus lived in Galilee. "Other-worldly religion did develop those ideas and those motives which served the salvation of the individual in the life to come, but it left many other talents of Christianity buried in a napkin."[23]

To the ordinary reader of the Bible. "inheriting the Kingdom of Heaven" means simply, being saved and going to heaven; for others the organized Church; and for others still, it means the invisible Church. For the mystic, it means the hidden life with God.

The Church is primarily a fellowship for worship; but the Kingdom, a fellowship for righteousness. The Church is only an agency to create the Kingdom of God, but practically it came to regard itself as the Kingdom."[24]

Part one of this chapter has been a study and a review in a fragmentary way, of the ideas and teachings of the Old Testament Hebrews; in it have been mentioned the conceptions that the primitive Israelitish tribes had, of the Kingdom of God; the broader views of the prophets and their convictions that the King wanted a righteous life in his subjects; also the beliefs of the Pharisees, of John the Baptist, of St. Paul, and of St. John, as well as the conceptions of the people, during the succeeding historical periods down to our present era.

[22]"I have no desire to disparage this type of religion. My own youth was nurtured in it and even its defects have something of a dearness to me, like the narrow staircases and sloping ceilings of an old home." *Christianizing the Social Order*, 75.
[23]*Christianizing the Social Order*, 75.
[24]*A Theology for the Social Gospel*, 134.

In part two, it is the purpose to study the Kingdom and Reign of God, according to Jesus' teachings, as Doctor Rauschenbusch presents them.

2

A The Teachings of Jesus Concerning The Kingdom of God

Jesus accepted John the Baptist as his fore-runner, and he shared the substance of the expectation of the Hebrews, but, as a true leader, he reconstructed, clarified, and elevated the hope of the masses. According to Dr. Rauschenbusch's conception, Jesus believed that the Kingdom, the true social order, is the highest good; all other good things are contained in it.

The whole aim of Jesus was a redemption of the entire social life of the human race. He spoke of this "great good" as the Kingdom of God, which was the pivot of his teachings, yet he nowhere defines the phrase. His audience needed no definition, as it was then a familiar phrase and conception. He took an understanding of it for granted with his hearers, and simply announced that it was now close at hand, and that they must act accordingly.

The new thing was simply that it was on the point of coming. The Kingdom of God is a master fact, yet Jesus did not mean merely a political kingdom or theocratic state. Neither did he use the term as a figure of speech, merely to indicate a perfect method of life for the individual.

He said the Kingdom of God was his fatherland, in which his spirit lived with God; yet, "he never transferred the kingdom hope from earth to heaven, nor did he ever spiritualize the vitality out of it, as the Church has so constantly done."[25]

[25] *Social Principles of Jesus,* 58.

He sent out the twelve with this message: "As ye go, preach, saying, the Kingdom of Heaven is at hand."[26]

"The idea covered by the phrase was an historic product of the Jewish people and we shall have to understand it as such."[27] But, under his hands, the Jewish imperialistic dream changed into a call for universal fraternity, and Jesus clearly demonstrated the fact that the Kingdom of God is not a triumph of Judaism.

On the other hand, nothing could be more contrary to the teachings of Jesus than the "vulgar notion that he fixed his attention on another world."[28] His ministry was for this life here on earth. He was gladly surrendering home, comfort, public approval and life itself, to realize the Reign of God in humanity.

Furthermore, the pious Jew expected God to enforce the ceremonial law, but Jesus had little to say about religious ceremonial, and a great deal about righteousness and love. He himself, was so indifferent to the ceremonial laws that he "struck the earnest religionists of his day as a man of loose life and of destructive influence."[29]

In the sermon on the Mount, Jesus formally outlined his conceptions of ethical and religious life, as distinguished from those then current. It was the "platform of the Kingdom of God."[30]

All who felt the divine dissatisfaction with themselves, and the craving for social righteousness and for justice, would get their satisfaction; but the climax of praise and promise, is for those who propagated righteousness where it was not wanted, and suffered for it.

"Jesus evidently felt deeply the emptiness and futility of much of the religious talk. He was interested only in

[26] *Social Principles of Jesus*, 69. Matthew 10: 7.
[27] *Social Principles of Jesus*, 57.
[28] *Ibid.*, 50.
[29] *Christianizing the Social Order*, 61.
[30] *Social Principles of Jesus*, 56.

those emotions and professions which could get themselves translated into character and action."[31]

While he had deep reverence and loyalty for the religion of his nation, "never advising his followers to break with it," yet he asserted boldly that the customary ethics of Judaism based on the Decalogue and its interpretation by the Jewish theologians, were not good enough. It needed to be "fulfilled and to have its lines prolonged."[32]

The popular leaders of society, the able, the educated, the powerful, were concerned in setting up their own kingdom, and enslaving their fellows as servants. So Jesus took what material he had, among the poor such as peasants and fishermen, and created a new leadership.

The Jewish conception of God was cast in the mold furnished by human despotism; but when Jesus spoke of the Hebrew Jehovah as our "Father," he democratized God and His Kingdom.

"By raising the value of the human soul and its life on the one side, and by bringing God down close to us as our Father, he laid the religious foundation for modern democracy and anticipated the craving of the modern spirit."[33]

In the Synagogue at Nazareth, he set forth the program of the Kingdom from Isaiah; it meant glad news to the poor; release to the captives; sight to the blind and liberty to bruised and crushed lives.

He put all who sought entrance to the Kingdom, under the law of love and service. Jesus initiated the Kingdom by his own life work, which was one of continual social service, and his own death was the greatest expression of love.

"The Kingdom of God is a fellowship of righteousness. Moreover, the establishment of a community of righteousness in mankind, is just as much a saving act of God, as

[31]*Ibid.*, 67.
[32]*Ibid.*, 89.
[33]*Christianizing the Social Order*, 61-62.

the salvation of an individual from his natural selfishness and moral inability."[34] It is the purpose of God to lift the human race, and every human life is so placed that it can share with God in the creation of the Kingdom, or it can resist and retard its progress."[35]

By accepting it as a task, we experience it as a gift, and by laboring for it we enter into the joy and peace of the Kingdom as our divine fatherland and habitation."[36]

The Kingdom of God is humanity organized according to the will of God, and at every stage of human development, it tends toward a social order which will best guarantee to all personalities, their freest and highest development.

"The Kingdom of God, as Jesus taught, is not confined within the limits of the Church and its activities. It embraces the whole human life and it is the Christian transfiguration of the social order."[37] Love to God and Love to man, is the sole outlet for the energy of religion. We rarely sin against God alone. When we democratize the conception of the King, then the definition of sin will have become more realistic. We love and serve God when we love and serve our fellows, whom He loves.

The social Gospel of Jesus teaches us, "to prize liberty and to love Jesus."[38] Today it is the social gospel which has the democratic outlook and sense of solidarity.

To Jesus, the Kingdom of God was both present and future, and he was filled with that consciousness that God is in human affairs on earth as well as in the affairs of heaven.

"An outlook toward the future in which the 'spiritual

[34] *A Theology for the Social Gospel*, 140.
[35] *A Theology for the Social Gospel*, 141.
[36] *Ibid.*
[37] *Ibid.*, 145.
[38] *Ibid.*, 177.

Conceptions of the Kingdom of God 41

life' is saved and the economic life is left unsaved, is both un-Christian and stupid."[39]

Though we derive our belief in a future life from the resurrection of Christ, his teachings and the common faith of the Christian Church, there is no inherent contradiction whatever, between the hope of the progressive development of mankind toward the kingdom of God on earth, and the hope of the consummation of our personal life in an existence after death.

It is our business to Christianize both expectations. The desire for Heaven attains Christian dignity and quality, only when it arises on the basis of that solidaristic state of mind which is cultivated by the social gospel. We want the possiblity of growth and cannot conceive of finite existence or human happiness, except in terms of growth. How can we then become more Christlike on earth or in Heaven, except by love and service?

In this second part of the present chapter, it has been pointed out that Jesus' conception of the Kingdom, and his teachings concerning it were:

(1) That it is a Fraternity of righteousness, service and love. (2) That "Our universe is not a despotic monarchy with God above the starry canopy and ourselves down here; but it is a spiritual commonwealth, with God in the midst of us."[40] (3) That it is not a "post mortem" condition only. Jesus believed the Kingdom of God to be both present and future, and that God permeated the human affairs of earth.

(4) That it means the salvation of the community as well as of the individual. (5) That salvation, growth and solidarity are conditional on interchange of service. (6) "That the worth of personality, freedom, growth, love, solidarity, service, these are the marks of the King-

[39] *A Theology for the Social Gospel*, 224.
[40] *Ibid.*, 49.

dom of God. (7) That our labor for the Kingdom here, will be our preparation for our participation hereafter."⁴¹ (8) "That the Kingdom, the true social order, is the highest good; all other good things are contained in it."⁴²

The aim in Part B. is to take up as Doctor Rauschenbusch taught them, the three fundamental social principles of Jesus, applied in general, during his stay on earth.

B   Three Fundamental Principles of Jesus

(1)   The Value of Life

The respect of Jesus for every person whom he met was due to his religious insight into human life and destiny. With him, the consciousness of a God of Love revealed the beauty of men. They were all children of that God and even the lowliest was high. The light that shone on him from the face of God, shed a splendor on the prosaic ranks of men.

That sense of sacredness is the basis for the whole missionary and philanthropic activity of Christian men and women, and where the Church really spread the Christian sense of the worth and sacredness of human life, it has been a great stabilizer of civil liberty.

The principle of reverence for personality is the ruling principle in ethics and in religion; it constitutes therefore, the truest and highest test of either an individual or a civilization.

To inflict on anyone either bodily or spiritual injury, revealed to Jesus, inexpressible guilt. Wherever he healed the sick, he rendered a social service to his fellows, and the spontaneous tendernesss which he put into his contact

⁴¹*A Theology for the Social Gospel*, 239.
⁴²*Social Principles of Jesus*, 53.

Conceptions of the Kingdom of God 43

with them, was an expression of his sense of the sacredness of life.

The horror which Jesus felt for the abuse of man by words of contempt, is an expression of his own respect for the worth of personality, and he was here for social restoration and moral salvation of those who were thus abused.

He was not only willing to help people who came to him for help, but he proposed to go after them. "No human being should go to pieces if he could help it."[43]

And so, "The deeper our insight into human destiny becomes, the more sacred does every individual human being seem to us."[44]

We shall be at one with the spirit of Christianity and modern civilization, if we approach all men with the expectation of finding beneath commonplace, sordid, or even repulsive externals, some qualities of love, loyalty, heroism, aspiration, or repentance which proves the divine in man."[45]

(2) The Solidarity of the Human Family

Men belong Together

This is the second of Jesus' principles in relation to society. He believed in the solidarity of the human family. Love is the social instinct which binds man and man together and makes them indispensable to one another. Jesus felt this solidarity of the neighborhood groups in Galilee with whom he mingled, and he treated them as composite personalities jointly responsible for their moral decisions. His love and respect were real and genuine.

We know that by constant common action, a social group develops a common spirit and common standards of

[43]*The Social Principles of Jesus*, 5.
[44]*Ibid.*, 9.
[45]*Ibid.*, 14.

action, which then assimilate and standardize the actions of the members of its group.

The natural social instinct of human affection is intensified and uplifted by religious motives and forces, and it is the special function of Christians to promote social unity and thus expand its blessings.

"Jesus himself was personally very sociable and enjoyed mixing with people. The denial of Peter and the betrayal of Judas hurt him, partly because they were comrades of his group. In Gethesmane he craved friendship. While he prayed to God, he reached out for Peter and John."[46] The longing for friendship and the unrest of loneliness are proof of a truly human and social nature.

Because social unity was so important to Jesus, forgiveness was imperative. In the Lord's prayer he makes full fellowship with man, a condition for full fellowship with God. "Forgive us our debts as we have forgiven our debtors."[47]

No one felt this social unity of our race more deeply than Jesus, which to him, was sacred and divine. Anything that substituted antagonism for fraternity was evil to him.

"Just as in the case of the natural respect for human life and personality, so in case of the natural social cohesion of men, he lifted the blind instinct of human nature by the insight of religion, and constituted it a fundamental principle of life."[48]

Thus, the passionate loyalty with which an entire nation defends its country and its freedom, is not simply a defense of real-estate and live-stock, but a defense of its national brotherhood and solidarity—a defense prompted by love.

A world-wide civilization must have a common mono-

[46] *The Social Principles of Jesus*, 19.
[47] *Ibid., Matthew* 6: 12.
[48] *The Social Principles of Jesus*, 23.

Conceptions of the Kingdom of God

theistic faith as its spiritual basis, and such a faith must be unitive and not divisive. What the world needs now, is a religion with a powerful sense of solidarity. This requires forgiveness, not "Until seven times, but until seventy times seven times."[49]

In the midst of a world full of diverse selfishness, we as Christians are expected to accept the brotherhood of man as the ruling principle of our lives and undertake to put it into practice in our private and public activities. We dedicate our lives to establishing the Kingdom of God, and to winning mankind to its laws.

"We can observe the fact that personal discipleship with Christ has given many a rare capacity for love, a social sympathy, peaceableness, and genuine society-making qualities."[50]

(3) Standing With the People

The Strong Must Stand up for the Weak

This, the third great fundamental principle, formed another plank in the social platform of Jesus. He saw his own aims summarized in Isaiah, and he now announced it as his program. Its promises were now about to be realized. What were they? "Glad tidings for the poor, release for the imprisoned, freedom for the oppressed and a 'year of Jehovah'."[51]

Social and religious emancipation are woven together in these phrases. Plainly, Jesus felt his mission in raising to free and full life, those whom life had bound and held captive.

He loved these people, felt their worth, trusted their latent capacities and promised them the Kingdom of God.

[49]*Matthew*, 18: 21-22.
[50]*The Social Principles of Jesus*, 27.
[51]*The Social Principles of Jesus*, 32, Isaiah 61: 1-2.

The Messiah was expected to purge the people of evil elements, winnowing the chaff from the wheat and burning it, but Jesus manifested no such spirit. He the strong, was standing up for the weak. Human suffering was being relieved and the poor were having glad news proclaimed to them.

"The selection of the Twelve, their grouping by twos, and their employment as independent messengers, was the most important organizing act of Jesus, out of which ultimately grew the Christian Church."[52] The motives which led up to this organization, were Jesus' distress and sympathy for the oppressed and miserable. The people were like a flock of sheep after the wolves are through with them.

Everywhere Jesus was relieving social misery, 'Standing with the People'.

"Our own understanding of personal salvation itself is deeply affected by the new solidaristic comprehension furnished by the Social Gospel of Jesus."[53]

Wherever any group has developed real solidarity, its best attention is always given to those who are most in need, and in recent centuries the vast forces of social evolution seem to have set in the direction toward which Jesus faced.

The new historical interpretation of the Bible helps us to see him more plainly amid the social life of his own people, applying these three social principles. The first, "Life and Personality are Sacred;" the second, "Men Belong Together;" and the third, "The Strong Must Stand with the Weak and Defend Their Cause."

[52]*The Social Principles of Jesus*, 33.
[53]*A Theology for the Social Gospel*, 96.

CHAPTER V

HIS TEACHINGS CONCERNING RACE PREJUDICE AND CLASS DISTINCTION

Knowing now Jesus' conception of the Kingdom and his fundamental social principles it seems appropriate in the remaining chapters, to study how Doctor Rauschenbusch, either directly or indirectly, points out the connection between these principles and modern social problems.

It is recognized that not one of these problems can, in any absolute sense be dealt with entirely by itself, yet in a simple way, the attempt is made to review the prominent problems mentioned in his discussions.

There has probably never been an age in human history comparable to the present, in its capacity for appreciating these principles which are discovered beneath the words and conduct of Jesus.

The fundamental, ethical principles of Jesus were the direct outgrowth of his conception of the Kingdom of God, and only the persons having the substance of the Kingdom ideal in their minds, seem to be able to obtain real consolation out of the ethics of Jesus. Having had this ideal set before us, "in some germinal and rudimentary form, salvation turns us from a life centered on ourselves, towards a life going out toward God and man."[1]

If Jesus regarded every human life as sacred, if he believed in the solidarity of the human family, if he taught that the strong must stand up for the weak, and if in his doctrine of equality we are all brothers to Christ and to one another, then, of course there can be no room for race prejudice in the new social order; and if the principle of

[1] *A Theology for the Social Gospel*, 98.

reverence for personality and the need of solidarity are among the chief principles in ethics or religion, then in the Christian social order, there can be no class differences which surround the upper classes with honor, but depreciate the lower classes by contrast that neutralizes the feeling of sacredness in human life.

Jesus felt this sacredness of personality in its humblest and hard-worn form, and he felt the family unity of all races and people. Therefore he was concerned about the poor, the aliens, and the miserable, and therefore in the new social order, "there can be neither Jew nor Greek; there can be neither bond nor free."[2]

The social Gospel emphasizes the fact that God is the bond of racial unity. The equality of fraternity exists in the enjoyment and exercise of love; the reign of love tends toward the progressive unity of mankind, but with the maintenance of individual liberty and the opportunity of nations to work out their own national peculiarities and ideals. "The approximate social equality existing in our country in the past, has been one of the chief charms of life here and of far more practical importance to our democracy than the universal ballot."[3]

The God whom Jesus had within was not the God of one race; and the Gospels show us Jesus in the act of crossing the racial boundary lines and outgrowing nationalistic religion. He recognized the religious qualities, even in a pagan.

"The man who intelligently realizes the Chinese and the Zulu as his brothers, with whom he must share the earth, is an ampler mind, other things being equal—than the man who can think only in the terms of pale faces."[4] Regardless of color or rank, he is a brother to Spaniard and Moor, Kurd and Armenian, Serb and Bulgar.

[2]*Galatians*, 3: 28.
[3]*Christianity and the Social Crisis*, 248.
[4]*The Social Principles of Jesus*, 27.

In Jesus we recognize that spirit that beats down the trammels of a narrow group, to seek a wider allegiance that reaches out beyond the "jingo patriotism" toward the brotherhood of nations, and that smites race prejudice or pride in the face, in the name of humanity.[5]

Wherever the members of a social organization have accustomed themselves to calling one another brother, whether black or white, it has stood for highers ideals.

Social Christianity is adding to the variety of religious experience and is creating a new type of man who bears a striking likeness to Jesus of Galilee; a type that respects human personality in every individual.

In that great charter of social prayers, wherein Jesus bids us say, "Our Father," he spoke from that consciousness of human solidarity which was a matter of course in all of his thinking. He compels us to clasp hands in spirit with all of our brothers and thus approach the Father. This rules out all selfish isolation in race or religion. Before the All-seeing, man is surrounded by the spiritual throng of all to whom he stands related, near and far.

Even in the most wretched and the lowliest specimens of humanity, Jesus recognizes a sacred and valuable personality. That sense of sacredness is the basis for the whole missionary and philanthropic activity of Christian men and women.

It was the flow of Christ's feeling toward the less attractive masses of humanity, that opposed the assumption that the many are incapable or inferior, and the few, superior.

To be a servant is not to be any less a man. No more striking lesson of social equality was ever given, than that of Jesus washing the feet of his disciples.

Jesus was no discriminator of class or color, when he told the story of the Good Samaritan. In it he represents

[5]*Christianizing the Social Order*, 60.

the alien and the heretic as the good neighbor. He went out of his way to set up a Samaritan as a model of human kindness, above the priest and the Levite.

"That would be the same as if an American orator should tell an Illinois crowd of the superior virtues of the 'Dago' and the 'Hunk', or an Alabama crowd of the brotherhood of the negro."[6]

Following are extracts of Doctor Rauschenbusch's 'Prayer for the Immigrants', in which are revealed his deep sympathy for and personal interest in the foreigner.

"Oh Thou Champion of the outcast....we remember before thee, the people of other nations who are coming to our land seeking bread, a home, and a future. May we look with thy compassion upon those who have been drained and stunted by the poverty and oppression of centuries, and whose minds have been warped by superstition or seared by the dumb agony of revolt.....We beseech thee that our republic may no longer fail her trust.... In a nation dedicated to liberty, may these strangers not find the old oppression and a fiercer greed.......Make thou our great commonwealth once more a sure beacon-light of hope and a guide on the path which leads to the perfect union of law and liberty.'"[7]

The social principle of Jesus, that 'the strong must stand up for the weak' aligned him with all men who are working for a nation with fraternal institutions, fraternal national consciousness, and for a coming family of nations and races.

As to classism, Doctor Rauschenbusch teaches that approximate equality is the only enduring foundation of political democracy; and the sense of equality is the only basis for Christian morality. He furthermore says that social equality *can* co-exist with natural differences. This is strikingly evident in a college community where there are "various gradations of rank and authority within the faculty; but there is social equality. On the other

[6]*Christianizing the Social Order*, 60.
[7]*Prayers of the Social Awakening*, 59.

hand, the janitor and the peanut vender are outside the circle, however important they may be to it."⁸

Individual sympathy and understanding has been our chief reliance in the past, for overcoming the differences between the social classes. These feelings and principles implanted by Christianity have been a powerful aid in that direction, but if this sympathy diminishes by the widening of the social chasm, what hope have we?

Since the supreme law of Christ is love, the Kingdom of God implies a progressive reign of love even in political, industrial, and other social affairs.

The poor, the alien, the stranger and the outcast, need the championship of the strong.

"If we allow deep and permanent chasms of inequality to grow up in our country, it is as sure as gravitation, that not only the old democracy and frankness of manners will go, but even the theory of human equality which has been part of our spiritual atmosphere through Christianity will be denied."⁹

Every time Jesus met a Gentile, we can see the Jewish prejudices melt away and he gladly discovered the human brotherhood and spiritual capacity in the alien.

"He reminded the indignant audience at Nazareth, that the great Elijah had found his refuge with a heathen Phoenician and Elijah had healed only a Syrian leper. When one leper out of ten thanked Jesus, he took pains to point out that this one was a Samaritan foreigner."¹⁰

Pride disrupts society. Race prejudice creates chasms between nations and classes. Love equalizes and promotes social unity. Instead of a society resting on coercion, exploitation and inequality, Jesus desired to found a society resting on love, service and equality. When he said, 'Ye are the salt of the earth,' he spoke with the conscious-

⁸*Christianity and the Social Crisis*, 248.
⁹*Ibid.*, 253.
¹⁰*Christianity and the Social Crisis*, 61.

ness of an historic mission to the whole of humanity. Under the conviction of the principle that the 'strong must bear the burdens of the weak,' he placed upon the strong, the obligation to champion the cause of all whose life is impaired or whose place within humanity is denied. He planned to bring about the transition of the old order to the new, by exchanging the area of moral obligation and by raising the standards of moral relationships.

The teachings of Doctor Rauschenbusch on this subject as given in the present chapter are:—

(1) Jesus' principles lead us to turn from self to God and our fellowmen.
(2) His doctrine of equality leaves no room for race prejudice and class differences in the Christian social order.
(3) The equality of fraternity exists in the exercise of love extending to all nations and races.
(4) Social Christianity is creating a new type of man, that respects human personality in every individual.
(5) Jesus demonstrated the fact, that to be a servant is not to be any less a man.
(6) Approximate equality is the only basis for Christian morality.
(7) Deep chasms of inequality will endanger our democracy as to frankness of manners and to our Christian atmosphere.
(8) Jesus' plan was to expand the area of the old social order, to increase our moral obligations and to raise the standards of our moral relationship.

CHAPTER VI

PERSONAL DISTRIBUTION OF WEALTH

1

Wealth and its Pursuit

"All methods of wealth-getting in society can apparently be classified under two heads: first, the rendering of service to others or to society, for the sake of an adequate reward in return; and second, the acquirement of gain for one's self at the expense of others, with practically no service rendered to society."[1]

The latter methed used to be practiced by beggars, thieves, lords, courtesans and princes, but as Professor Jenks says, it is now practiced with success by stockholders. Business can get something for nothing; but Society cannot. If Business fails to pay its bills, somebody else farther down the line will have to settle up. What is 'easy money' for one man is bound to be hard loss to another, or to hundreds of others.

"Every 'get-rich-quick' concern is balanced by thousands of 'get-poor-quick' people who are still stupid enough to trust their fellow-men."[2]

Like all the greatest spiritual teachers of mankind, Jesus realized a profound danger to the better self, in the pursuit of wealth. In his desire to create a true human society, he encountered riches as a prime divisive force in actual life; and he taught us that wealth is apt to grow stronger than the man who owns it.

In Luke 12: 13-21, is shown his attitude toward the

[1]*Christianizing the Social Order*, 228.
[2]*Ibid.*

accumulator. When the rich man said: "Life, you have ample possessions laid up for many years to come; take your case, eat, drink, enjoy yourself," God said to him: "Foolish man, this night your life is demanded from you; and these preparations—for whom shall they be?"

Most men today would have no fault to find with the man in this parable, but unlimited acquisition used to be considered immoral and dishonorable. To Jesus the 'fat farmer' in that story was a tragic comedy. To plan life as if it consisted in an abundance of material wealth, is something of a miscalculation in a world where death is part of the scheme of things.

Property is intended to secure freedom of action and self-development, but it often chains men and clips their wings. This is what Jesus calls the 'deceitfulness of riches.'

Some of the dangers connected with the accumulation of wealth are these:

(1) It is hard to acquire great wealth without doing injustice to others; it is hard to possess it and yet deal with others on the basis of equality as to humanity. (2) "It is hard to give it away without doing mischief." "It is even hard to spend riches with love." (3) Wealth as Jesus saw it, flouted the value of life, dissolved the spiritual solidarity of whole classes and kept the lowly low; the wealthy had lost the capacity for an heroic life. He taught that riches have so fatal an attraction over the mind, that one's heart is sure to be bound up with his wealth. (4) In addition to the blight of character, wealth often exerts a desocializing and divisive influence. It wedges apart groups that belong together. It must be that a life given over to sumptuous living and indifferent to the want and misery of 'a fellow-man at the doorstep, seemed to Jesus a deeply immoral and sinful life, when he

Christianity and the Social Crisis, 77.

gave us the parable of the rich man and Lazarus. Jesus exerted his energies to bring men close together in love, but great riches divide and separate. (5) In the case of the young ruler, Jesus encountered the fact that wealth often bars men out of the world of their ideals. It creates semi-human relations between social classes, so that a small dole seems to be a full discharge of obligations toward the poor, and that manly independence and virtue may be resented as offensive.

"Jesus did not ask the rich young ruler to hand over his property for the common purse, as the church in later times did, but he simply told him to turn it back to social usefulness and come down to the common level."[4] (6) There is great danger in the power of wealth. The immense power wielded by the rich is an intoxicant that few can withstand permanently. We have individuals in our country so rich that it is practically inconceivable that they should be 'brought to book' and be punished like ordinary citizens, when they commit crime.[5]

Others among the greatest and most searching moral teachers of humanity have agreed with Jesus in his diagnosis of the classes that live on unearned wealth. They hold that its influence is demoralizing. (7) They also have claimed that wealth places men and women in moral danger, because it vastly increases the number of inferiors and decreases the number of equals with whom they can associate. It has been said that only our equals are in position to rebuff our conceit or rudeness and thus make our manhood grow straight.

Doctor Rauschenbusch says furthermore, that the wrongs connected with wealth are the most vulnerable point of our civilization. "Unless we can make that

[4]*Christianity and the Social Crisis*, 77.
[5]*Christianizing the Social Order*, 274.

crooked place straight, all our charities and religion are involved in hypocrisy."[6]

"In so far as rich men have been mere accumulators of unearned wealth, they need expect no praise from the future. There is nothing in ethics, in politics, or in economics that makes the swollen fortunes of our day desirable or admirable."[7]

Our system of private ownership has disconnected the power of the strong from the service of the community and has concentrated it on the accumulation of private wealth. The indirect good done through them might have been accomplished in more direct ways; but their evil results will gather force far into the future.

From now on, the great problem of statesmanship in the capitalistic nations, will be, how to stop the further accumulation of unearned wealth.[8] In so far as profit contains an ingredient which is gained without productive labor, at the expense of others, and without their consent, it is the highest duty of the Christian to aid society in tracing this parasitic tribute to its source, and in preventing its further absorption. This opposition is to be Christ-like.

In all probability there is not a single state in our Union which has not seen the reputation and financial or political standing of good men killed in cold blood, because they sincerely opposed high-class graft; whoever tries opposing it will suffer.

We shall not understand the problem of Christianizing the social order as long as we regard unchristianized Business as a passive object, to be molded into finer and nobler lines under our hands; for it is alive, vibrant, strong, assertive, impatient and full of fight.

"There has always been social misery, but while wealth

[6] *The Social Principles of Jesus*, 127.
[7] *Christianizing the Social Order*, 305.
[8] *Ibid.*

was multiplying beyond all precedent, an immense body of pauperism with all its allied misery, was growing up and becoming chronic."[9] Men learned to make wealth much faster than they learned to distribute it justly. Many times their eye for profit has been keener than their ear for the voice of God and humanity.

If our social order is to be Christianized, wealth by extortion must cease; work and service must become the sole title to income.

In so far as profit is only another name for the fair reward which society owes for useful labor and service, it has a sound moral basis.

Every honest and fair increase in income, really brings new and wholesome pleasure within reach. Men justly desire wealth because it will give them leisure to cultivate their intellectual life. And, in the true social order, the aim of private property should be to make an honest living, to give the children an education and a start in life; to 'lay up' something for the future and to rise a step in life, if possible; and, in so far as our present economic system is simply the perfection of human association, Christianity can have 'no quarrel with it."[10]

The moral problem to be solved by us is, how to safeguard the rights of the individual holder of property, who has increased its value by his labor and intelligence, and yet, to extract for the community the value which the community creates.

No nation can allow its natural sources of wealth to be owned by a limited and diminishing class without suffering political enslavement and poverty.

"The abolition of private property in land, in the interest of society, is a necessity."[11]

Moreover, since the industrial revolution, the man-made

[9] *Christianity and the Social Crisis*, 217.
[10] *Christianizing the Social Order*, 163.
[11] *Christianity and the Social Crisis*, 280.

machinery of production has assumed an importance formerly unknown; it is fully as important in the modern process of production, as the land from which the raw material is drawn. Consequently the chief way to enrichment in an industrial community, will be the control of these factors of production, by the community.

The desire for private property has been the chief outlet for selfish impulses which have often been detrimental and antagonistic to public welfare. In order to gain this wealth, men have slaughtered the forests, contaminated the rivers, drained the fertility of the soil, and monopolized the mineral wealth of the country. More than this they have enslaved childhood, double-yoked motherhood, and exhausted manhood, in their dealings with humanity for the sake of accumulation of riches. Jesus opposed accumulation without moral purpose, and the fatal absorption of money-making.

A simple acquaintance with human life will show us that private property is at the same time, a necessary expression of personality and stimulator of character, and, on the other hand a chief outlet and fortification of selfishness.[12]

In part one of this chapter, it has been the purpose to review as Doctor Rauschenbusch discusses it, the subject of "Wealth and its Pursuit." He emphasized the dangers and the wrongs in accumulating unearned wealth, and mentioned particularly the following:

(1) It is hard to acquire great wealth without injustice to others, and it is even harder to dispose of it wisely. (2) Jesus taught by his parables, that riches influence the soul, the heart and the will. (3) Few can withstand the intoxicating power of wealth. (4) Great accumulated wealth causes deep chasms between classes of people. (5) Jesus opposed accumulation of wealth with-

[12]*The Social Principles of Jesus*, 116.

out purpose. (6) The wrongs connected with wealth are the most vulnerable point of our civilization. (7) Our system of private ownership has disconnected the power of the strong from the service of the community. (8) The great problem of our statesmanship is how to stop further accumulation of unearned wealth. (9) When private property is used for the perfection of human association or for the comfort, health and education of the family—private ownership is on a sound basis. (10) Honest and fair increase in income is right. (11) The community should own the great factors of production, such as land and power-machinery.

2

The Rich, the Poor, the Criminal
and the Outcast

To the question, "Can a rich man be saved?" comes the reply: "It can be done but it takes a tremendously heroic cure to do it." In Matthew 19: 24, we are told that it is easier for a camel to go through the eye of a needle, than for a rich man to enter the Kingdom of Heaven.

Jesus saw in the actions of the rich young ruler, whom he loved in spite of his riches, a confirmation of his belief that it is well nigh impossible for a rich man to enter the higher life. The young man who was departing with clouded face was simply a demonstration of a general fact.[12]

[12]"In thus presenting the moral situation of the accumulation of unearned wealth, I have been free from any emotion of envy, class-hatred, or personal grudge. I have only good will and friendship for every rich man and woman I have ever met. Some were among the finest characters I have ever known. This is simply a modern exposition of Jesus' saying on the camel and the needle's eye." *Christianizing the Social Order*, 808.

Again Jesus was deeply moved when Zacchaeus who had a Roman franchise to collect the taxes of a wealthy district, did change his selfish habits and promised to make fourfold restoration of all his graft. Fifty percent of his property was given outright; the rest was used to make restitution at the rate of four hundred percent. "Here a camel passed through the needle's eye,"[14] and Jesus promptly made friends with Zacchaeus because of his determination to make restitution.

Jesus was by no means hostile to the rich, but he took the social view of salvation and that explains his doubts about the fitness of the rich to enter the Kingdom of God.

While the natural leaders of society, the rich and powerful, were busy setting up their kingdom among the aristocrats, Jesus, a poor carpenter selected the common people, peasants, fishermen and other laborers, and created a new system of a democratic order.

Any one studying life today, as it is, on the basis of real estate and bank clearings, would come to the conclusion that God is on the side of the rich, but "it takes a revelation to see it the other way."[15]

When we learn from the Gospels that God is on the side of the poor, and that he proposes to view anything done or not done to them as having been done or not done to him, such a revelation of solidarity comes with a regenerating shock to our selfish minds. Jesus stood for the rights of the helpless; the widows and the fatherless were those who had no concrete power to back their claims; no influence, no financial standing, no 'pull' with the policemen.

The stranger was the immigrant who had no part in the blood kinship of the clan and hence no share in the land and no voice in the common affairs of city or village.

Even Old Testament Law, as well as the preaching of

[14]*The Social Principles of Jesus*, 68.
[15]*A Theology for the Social Gospel*, 168.

the prophets, manifest a striking sympathy for the poorer classes and an unflagging respect for their equal humanity. The manhood of the poor was more sacred to them than the property of the rich.

The common people heard Jesus gladly, because he said what appealed to their hearts. Having himself worked as a carpenter for years, there was nothing in his thinking to neutralize the sense of solidarity which grows up under such circumstances.

In Jesus' attitude toward the poor, as he set them over against the rich, he always saw the two groups of human society—those who live by their own productive labor and those who live on the productive labor of others whom they control.[16]

When we gain our perspective from a sufficient distance, we can distinguish the setting for Jesus' championship of the common folk. He always acted from a sense of the worth of the human life with which he was dealing, and this principle prompted him to be courteous and just, even to the criminal and the outcast.

When the Pharisees brought in the woman taken in adultery, who was listening to their accusation and who was going through the most harrowing experiences conceivable, exposed to the gaze of a leering and scornful crowd, Jesus shielded her from stoning, by the power of his personality and his consummate skill in controlling men.

With her good name torn away, and self-respect crushed, Jesus managed the embarrassing situation with gentlemanly tact, and when he was alone with her, what a mingling of kindness with severity there was![17]

Jesus showed respect for her personality even when she was in disgrace, and dealt with her courteously. Physical

[16]*The Social Principles of Jesus*, 40.
[17]*Ibid*, 8.

deformity or moral guilt could not obscure the divine worth of human life, to Jesus. To express contempt for any human being, was to him a horrible guilt.

No doubt the quotation from Isaiah 61: 1, was a favorite one with Jesus, as he brought glad tidings to the poor, sight to the blind and freedom to the oppressed. He brought not only glad tidings but happy realities. Neither did he over-look or forget the out-cast. This is illustrated in Matthew 8: 1-4.

When he came down from the mountain, behold, a leper came to him saying, 'Lord if thou wilt thou canst make me clean.' And Jesus stretched forth his hand, and actually touched him saying, 'I will, be thou clean.' The spontaneous tenderness which Jesus put into his contact with the sick or the outcast, was an expression of his sense of the sacredness of life. A leper with fingerless hands and decaying joints was repulsive to the aesthetic feelings and a menace to selfish fear of infection, therefore the community quarantined them in a waste place and stoned them when they crossed the bounds.

Jesus not only healed this man, but his sense of humanity so went out to him, that he stretched forth his hands and touched him!"[13] Even the most wretched specimen of the poor still had a value to him, whether he was physically miserable or morally degraded.

In every Jewish community, there was a fringe of unchurched people who were cast out because they could not keep up the strict observance of the law, and had seemingly given up trying. The pious people, just because they were pious, felt that they must ignore or treat these outcasts with scorn. Jesus walked across the lines thus established and associated with these publicans and sinners in order to help them.

In the Sermon on the Mount, Jesus demanded that the

[13]*The Social Principles of Jesus*, 8.

standards of social morality be changed and raised to a new level. He proposed that the feeling of anger and hate be treated as seriously as murder under the old code. To abuse a person, though he be a criminal or sinner, with words of contempt, denies his worth, breaks down his self-respect, and robs him of the regard of others.

When Jesus was among sinners, he accepted their invitations to dine with them, or he invited himself to their homes, thereby incurring the sneer of the respectable, as a friend of publicans, and a glutton and wine-drinker.

Although Jesus was a friend of all, and especially kind and sympathetic toward the poor and the sinner, his teachings were not that we must dispense with courts of law and safeguards for society against the socially destructive forces of unrestrained ignorance and vice or the disintegrating forces of evil.[19]

He taught however, that the law of love transcends all other laws, and that the instinct of love is a truer guide than all machine-made rules of charity or correction.

The law of love for one's neighbor applies to all, rich or poor, the sick, the criminal, the stranger and the outcast, as well as the respectable, influential and generally lovable.

In part two of this chapter are given scriptural examples used by Doctor Rauschenbusch to illustrate that:—

(1) Jesus was by no means hostile to the rich, although he constantly championed the cause of the poor; selected the common people for his followers and became their leader.

(2) He bore the burdens of the weak, and considered the life of even the most wretched persons as sacred.

(3) He was courteous and fair to the criminal and the degraded.

[19]*Luke* 20: 22-25.

(4) Physical deformity and moral guilt could not obscure the divine worth of any human being, to Jesus.

(5) He associated with publicans and sinners, with the poor and the outcast, in order to relieve them of their misery.

(6) Jesus did not oppose courts of law, and safeguards against the socially destructive forces of unrestrained ignorance, vice and evil, but he taught that the law of love transcends all other laws.

CHAPTER VII

A REVIEW OF THE PRESENT SITUATION
IN THE INDUSTRIAL WORLD

1

Employer versus Employee
Labor versus Wages
Profit versus Life

The discussions in this chapter will be mainly in the form of criticisms by Doctor Rauschenbusch on the present condition of our economic order, resulting from the great industrial revolution of the nineteenth century.

The American Declaration of Independence in 1776, and the French Revolution in 1789, signalized the birth of modern democracy. At about the same time however, another revolution came, which over-shadowed these great events.

With the arrival of the power-machine, the old economic world tottered and fell; the old customs and regulations which had forbidden or limited free competition, were brushed aside and new economic theories were developed. They sanctioned what was going on, and secured the support of public opinion and legislation for those who were driving the machine through the frame-work of the entire social structure.[1]

Industrial revolution has slowly spread, reaching not only one trade after another, but one nation after another and creating two classes, with a wide gulf between them. On the one hand, the employer and on the other, the wage-earner.

[1]*Christianity and the Social Crisis*, 213.

Disintegration of the old economic life brought about the possibility of working with head-long speed by means of the new machine, and it choked the market with its own goods and stopped its own wheels with the great mass of its output. Periodical prostrations of industry resulted, creating the dreaded distress of displeased workers.

The machine now compelled population to settle about it, thus becoming the creator of the modern crowded city. It piled the poor together in dirty tenements at night and in unsanitary factories during the day.[a] Poverty and filth leaped forward simultaneously with wealth.

It is hardly likely that any social revolution, by which capitalism may be over-thrown, will cause more injustice, more physical suffering, and more heart-ache, than the industrial revolution by which capitalism rose to power.[b]

The very instrument by which all humanity could rise from want and fear of want, actually submerged multitudes of our people in perpetual want and fear. This is especially true of the wealthiest countries, and it is a clear demonstration of the facts that the moral forces in humanity failed to keep pace with its intellectual and economic development.

Men learned to make wealth much faster than they learned to distribute it justly.

A   Employer *versus* Employee

The employer or business man is the seat of power and he sustains three relations to his fellow-men in the organism of business life: namely, the relation to other men of his own class with whom he competes or associates, the relation to the workers whom he employs, and the relation to the consumers whom he supplies.

[a] *Christianity and the Social Crisis*, 274.
[b] *Ibid.*, 218.

(1) In so far as modern business life has wrought out effective methods of associating workers into friendly co-operation it is good. Where such a system has prevailed, love has found an organized expression and the capacity for mutual understanding and good will is strengthened. Cooperation is not only morally attractive but economically effective. Competition may be a stimulant of sales, but cooperation is the life of the whole economic process. It is both moral and efficient.[4]

The application of this social principle is still limited to small areas and territories, and where one business firm collides with another of the same kind, we generally find that all the virtues or vices of war are developed. Most competitors conceal their methods, their markets, their prices and their plans, like the generals of contending armies. "Some department stores even have an organized spy-system to see that their rivals offer no special bargains, without being followed and countered."[5]

Often where competition has full sway, the aim is to capture the other man's trade, and to put him out of business. Thus, competition represses good-will and calls out selfishness and jealousy, even among Christian business men.

If a Methodist grocer stocks up a place on the corner opposite his Baptist competitor, will the Baptist pray God to bless his Methodist brother in his new business? Will the Methodist pray that his fellow Christian may continue to prosper?

The moral instinct of men has always condemned competitive selfishness and the man who sacrifices social solidarity for private gain. "The reign of competition is a reign of fear, and as a result, the rate of mortality for small business concerns, is higher than infant mortality."[6]

[4] *Christianizing the Social Order*, 170.
[5] *Christianizing the Social Order*, 171.
[6] *Ibid.*, 173.

Fear makes business men lie and cheat. "In commercial competition the worst man sets the pace and good men follow, because they are afraid."⁷ Often clean, kindly, religious men stoop to methods tricky, hard, rapacious, to which they are constantly driven by the pressure of business necessity, and of which they are ashamed. Men who have the finer moral discernment, do not want to do these things, but they are infected by the greed of commercial competition, through the medium of fear.

(2) Wherever our social order has been modernized and industrialized, the two distinct classes always confront each other, and the relation between the two is the moral problem of our age. On the one side are those who live by their own productive labor, and on the other are those who live on the productive labor of others who are under their control. Practically, they overlap and blend; each conditions the other, neither could exist without the other, but despotism is the permanent temptation of the strong, since they can own the property without which industry cannot go on.⁸ Labor depends upon capital, not only for bread but for the very chance to work for bread.

The corporation which is fast becoming the agency through which our large affairs are managed, was probably invented by Satan. It is, "as every lawyer knows, an artificial person begotten by the Law," and composed of many individuals "with powers greater and less than the sum of all its parts."⁹ It is created for profit, and gets its life, its intellect and its size by profit. It has an acquisitive mind, but no heart of pity, nor bowels of compassion. Though a given employer may regard his

⁷*Ibid.*
⁸*The Social Principles of Jesus,* 40; *Christianity and the Social Crisis,* 216; *Christianizing the Social Order,* 226, 180; *Prayers of the Social Awakening,* 61, 63.
⁹*Christianizing the Socal Order,* 184.

workmen with genuine human affection, yet all his business interests bid him regard them as mere units of labor, making money for him.[10]

So far as our civilization treats men merely as labor force, fit to produce wealth for the few, it is not yet Christian.[11]

Even where labor is strong and well organized, it is like a man holding up a heavy piece of timber by his hands, with every muscle tense and the perspiration running down his body.

Our continent from ocean to ocean, testifies to the willingness and capacity of the laborer, provided he has a chance and a motive to work. But in our own country powerful associations of employers have united to cripple and suppress the organization of labor.

The relation of employer and employee is still frankly undemocratic and every business concern is a little monarchy. It may be a just and benevolent one, but not based on freedom and equal rights.

Business is the last intrenchment of autocracy. Men have tasted democracy and found it good, therefore the industrial unrest. It is not due to the 'badness' of men, but "to their relish and hunger for applied Christianity."

"If any one doubts whether the violence of the working class is due to repression, let him read the history of trade unions and of socialism."[12] In industry we need a constitutional increase of freedom and power for the working class, even more than we need good and kind employers. As long as the happiness of the workers rests on the personal character of employers, it is insecure. Therefore we must set our faces toward a thorough-

[10]*Christianizing the Social Order*, 186.
[11]*The Social Priciples of Jesus*, 14.
[12]*Christianizing the Social Order*, 192.

going change in the relation between the two great economic classes.[13]

(3) In relation to the consumer, the business man is the steward of our national household. Innumerable business men have managed their business in such a way that they have the sincere liking and esteem of their customers, but in general, there is no solidarity between buyer and seller. Business is not carried on primarily to supply men with wholesome goods, but to make profit for the dealer, and the unwritten law of custom, leaves the seller ample room to tamper with the goods furnished.

Adulterated goods, falsely adjusted scales, short measures, are ancient and yet up-to-date devices. Very often the goods sold are actually harmful to the buyer. The entire liquor trade is an example of such an industry maintained by hook or by crook because it is profitable; but the immense profits bear down all considerations of humanity. Alcohol is a spirit born of the devil, but he is merely a satellite and a tool of a far greater devil, and that is Mammon.[14]

"The Pure Food and Drug Act transformed the labels of patent medicines, and the 40 percent of alcohol or 5 percent of opium, about which they had been so discreetly silent, leered out at last."[15] But this Act was bitterly fought by some of the interests concerned. The poisoning of the people must be done on a large scale or it does not pay. If dishonesty is forced on business by the public, as many claim, why does business fight for the right to be dishonest?[16]

If commerce existed to satisfy the economic needs of the consumers, it would keep pace with their needs. But since its chief aim is to make profits for the dealer, it out-

[13]*Christianizing the Social Order*, 199.
[14]*Ibid.*, 209.
[15]*Christianizing the Social Order*, 209.
[16]*Ibid.*, 213.

runs the actual needs. Even in its respectable forms, business often seeks to batter down all self-respect, and our self-restraint or power to resist. For example, the present craze for automobiles is not a spontaneous folly of the people, but "it is carefully worked up by the commercial interests."[17] Now the automobile is a highly valuable invention, but when men and women mortgage their homes, or surrender the chances of educating their children, in order to purchase a motor-car, they inflict a spiritual damage on themselves and the whole nation.

The generation now growing up, is lacking in that stern faculty of self-restraint, which was ground into its parents by religion and education. Capitalism is disintegrating that virtue of the preceding generation and is persuading the people to buy baubles so that capital can make profits. It is thus sapping its own foundations."[18] The ruling passion of Business puts the business man to a test, from which his personal character does not always emerge undamaged.

"Whatever moral goodness there is—and there is a great deal of it—comes through the fundamental soundness of human nature that insists on being kindly and fraternal;"[19] also through the fact that the main economic needs are clean and wholesome, and give moral worth to the work that supplies them.

Generally speaking, income depends on valuable service rendered, but if profit can be made best by neglecting the needs of the public, or even by damaging the life and health of the public, then that becomes the policy of Business.

[17]*Ibid.*, 211.
[18]Christianizing the Social Order, 211.
[19]*Ibid.*, 214.

B Labor *versus* Wages

Since the arrival of the power machine, the weary hum of the hand-spindle and the pounding of the hand-loom have practically ceased. With the rapid change of working equipments, came the serious conditions resulting from unfair adjustment of work and wages. "If the rich had only what they earned, and the poor had all they earned, all wheels would revolve more slowly and life would be more sane."[20]

Under the old system the working-man owned at least the simple tools of his trade, but today, few laborers have any part or lot in the machinery with which they work. The rule is, that a small group owns all of the material factors of land and machinery, while a large group owns nothing but the personal factor of human labor power.

Our blessings have failed to bless us, because they were not based on justice and solidarity. Our business life is the seat and source of our present troubles, especially where the power-machine has reduced the position of the laborer merely to feeding and attending to the machinery.

This wonderful product of human ability and toil, with its immense powers of production, has gravitated into the ownership and control of a relatively small class of men, "while a laborer may work twenty years for a corporation and contribute the most valuable service in building it up, yet have no part in it at the end."[21] Moreover, he is liable to be dismissed at any time. What is more pathetic than to see a poverty-stricken man arriving at old age without any means of support?[22]

[20] *Christianity and the Social Crisis*, 268.
[21] *Christianizing the Social Order*, 164.
[22] *Christianity and the Social Crisis*, 237.

C. Profit *versus* Life

Seldom is the attempt made to allot to each workman his share in the profits of the joint work. He is paid a fixed wage and the increase of this wage is limited only by the productiveness of his work; the decrease of it is limited only by the willingness of the workman to work at so low a return, which willingness is determined by his needs. Most often, the less he needs, the more he will receive, and the more he needs the less he will receive.

It is crushing to all proper pride, for a working man to be out of work for weeks, offering his work and his body and soul at one place after another, and to be told again and again that no one has any need of him.

"The purchasing power of the wages determines the health and the comfort of the working man and his family."[23] It does not determine the justice of the wage, which ought to be paid according to the total product of his work.

Though the laborer has doubtless profited to some extent with the increase of the nation's wealth, and perhaps now enjoys luxuries which were beyond the reach of the richest in former times, the bulk of the increase in wealth has gone to a limited class who in various ways have been strong enough to take it. "Wages have advanced on foot; profits have taken the Limited Express."[24]

The competitive necessities of industry, crowd people together in the cities into districts where there is lack of space, air and light. High rents force the working-man into small tenement houses with poor ventilation. Coal smoke and gas induce susceptibility to throat and lung diseases which develop into tuberculosis, and this spreads rapidly among the underfed and over-worked multitudes who live in densely populated quarters.

[23] *Christianity and the Social Crisis*, 233.
[24] *Ibid.*

Another drawback is the artificial rise in food prices, at the expense of the vital force of the American people. City life with the noises and strains, the hurry for trains, the contagious rush, is itself a flaring consumer of nervous energy.[25] The work at the machine brings additional rush and confusion of mind. Under such a combination of causes, the health of the people inevitably breaks down. Poorly fed and poorly housed, during the years when a working man's family is growing up, before their earnings become available, they are often submerged into poverty, and neither parents nor growing children are likely to escape physical degeneration.

Aside from the natural physical decline of the working people, it is their lot to suffer from mangling and mutilation. Industrial accidents have multiplied with the spread of the power-machine.[26] Power-hammers and lathes have a very different way of inflicting an injury from the old hammer and chisel of the former system, but Capitalism has been backward and even obstinate about adapting machinery to protect the safety of the workers. Unless the machinery is surrounded with proper safe-guards, it becomes a menace to life and limb. "We have never yet dared to get the facts, according to figures, for our country, except those in mining and railroading," but "it is safe to say, that no country is so reckless of accidents as our own."[27] It has been asserted that one in eight of our people dies a violent death. Many are injured in railway work and elsewhere, because long hours in the service of those corporations have so worn them out, that they were unable to save themselves.

The existence of a large number of laborers without any property rights in the material they work upon and in the tools they work with, and without any claim to the

[25]*Christianity and the Social Crisis*, 241.
[26]*Christianizing the Social Order*, 245.
[27]*Christianity and the Social Crisis*, 243.

profits resulting from their work, is bound to have subtle and far-reaching effects on the character of this class and on the moral tone of the people at large.

A man expresses himself in his work, as for instance, an artist or a professional man who takes pride in his production, or as the pleasure a housewife takes in adorning her home. But in many cases the laborer's surroundings are ugly, depressing and coarsening. Much of the material he is manufacturing, is an adulteration as to quality, made to sell rather than to serve. The making of such cotton or woolen lies, must react on the morals of every person who handles them. Under these conditions the modern factory-hand is not apt to develop artistic gifts. Why should he take an interest in his work, or put love and care into it when it is not his? He feels keenly that our system has made the immense majority of industrial workers mere hirelings.[28] The finest work is done only by free minds who put love into their work because it is their own. As soon as a workman becomes a partner, he becomes enthusiastic and works with renewed energy. Even a small bonus helps to spur him on.

When the average working-man's family is only a few weeks removed from destitution, his only incentive to work is fear of losing his 'job'. Thus, often the entire life for employer as well as for employee, is a reign of fear. It is only too true that a workman in his prime is always in danger of losing his position, but when he grows old, he is almost certain to lose it. This constant insecurity and fear pervading the entire condition of the laboring people, "like a corrosive chemical that disintegrates their self-respect," causes much of this industrial unrest.[29]

Wherever work is scarce, petty crime is plentiful. Every great strike, every industrial crisis, pushes some

[28]*Christianity and the Social Crisis*, 234; *The Social Principles of Jesus*, 14.
[29]*Christianity and the Social Crisis*, 237.

man over the line of self-respect into thievery or vagrancy.

Because accepting charity is at first one of the most bitter experiences of the self-respecting working-man, he will abandon his family or go insane or commit suicide, rather then surrender his independence.

The interests of the worker revolves around his job, for a job is his only chance to apply his working force, and his working force is all he has. "So the job is his sole hold on life, and his entire system of ethics becomes job-centric. To get a job, to hold it against those who might take it from him, and to make it yield him as much as possible of pay, leisure and comfort, is the absorbing concern of his soul."[30]

Another disintegrating influence generated by our system is hatred. The employers are often annoyed at the organizations of their men and the employees are angry with smouldering resentment at their treatment by the employers.

The economic loss on both sides in every strike is great enough, but the loss in human fellowship and kindliness, is of far greater moment. "Strikes are mild civil war, and war is hell."[31]

Nothing so holds down the rise of the working-man, as the dragging fringe of unemployed workers.

"If our industrial organization cannot evolve some saner method of reconciling conflicting interests, than 24,000 strikes and lockouts in twenty years, it will be a confession of social impotence and moral bankruptcy."[32] The best work on this baffling question, has been done by the labor-unions, and this alone would justify their existence."[33]

[30]*Christianizing the Social Order*, 165.
[31]*Christianity and the Social Crisis*, 239.
[32]*Ibid.*
[33]*Christianizing the Social Order*, 452.

The rise of the working-class involves an increase in their share of the profits of business. Capital should have its fair return, but the other factors of industry should get their share of the social dividend by increased wages and lower prices. As consumers, the wages-earners are concerned the same as all others, in receiving honest goods at fair prices. A maximum working day and a legal minimum of safety and comfort in the conditions of shop and mine labor, are a step toward a Christian social order.

If they are to rise to even worth with the other social classes, they must have the security and moral stimulus of property rights.[34] "The right to property is a corollary of the right to life; without property, men are at the mercy of nature and in bondage to those who have property."[35]

The man who lives only on his labor, is brought into social competition with people who have additional income through rents and profits, and "must break his back merely to keep his wife and children on a level with others."[36]

Social insurance against industrial accidents, occupational disease and old age, would act as a property right and would save the working-man from dropping into the bottomless pit of poverty and from the constant fear of it.[37]

We need a connected system of employment bureaus, such as the older countries have, but it must be controlled by the class it is to serve and not by those who are opposed to it.

Many of the workmen are hungry for intellectual food. To these, men and women of the professional classes can

[34]*Christianizing the Social Order*, 452.
[35]*The Social Principles of Jesus*, 127.
[36]*Christianity and the Social Crisis*, 268.
[37]*Ibid.* (1)

render valuable services. Every laborer should have enough technical education to understand the productive process of which he is a part.[38] The eight hour day and the work-less Sunday, would be sure aids to their intellectual development.

"Public opinion and the law must uphold the working class in their demand for collective bargaining."[39] This, in the long run, will likewise prove to be an advantage to the capitalist class.

In the future, too, the working-class can secure equal justice in the political field, by a readjustment of political power; now, the business class is in control. "The Socialist Party represents the point of view and interests of the working-class, just as accurately as the old parties have represented Capitalism."[40]

Before the outbreak of the Great War, it seemed safe to anticipate that the working-people would secure an increasing share of the social wealth, the security and the opportunities for health, for artistic enjoyment, and of that which makes life worth living, but today the future is clouded and uncertain.[41] We cannot make such progress toward a just social order, as long as the masses of working people in the industrial nations continue in economic poverty and political helplessness, and as long as the minority controls the land, the tools and the political power.[42]

We must trust to the modern spirit of democracy and the political grip of our grandchildren, to deal with the centipede of Labor, as we now have to deal with the octopus of Capital.[43]

Cooperation is the way of salvation, and its effectiveness

[38]*Christianizing the Social Order*, 452.
[39]*Ibid.*, 453. [40]*Ibid.*, 454.
[41]*The Social Principles of Jesus*, 42.
[42]*Ibid.*, 145.
[43]*Christianizing the Social Order*, 455.

has been amply demonstrated in the older countries; but it requires a strong sense of solidarity, loyalty and good faith to succeed. Insurance and cooperation are two great demonstrations of the power of solidarity. "In insurance, we bear one another's burdens, and so fulfill the law of Christ."[44]

It was the principle of the sacredness of life and personality that aligned Jesus with all idealistic minds to whom man is more than matter and more than labor force. It aligned him with all exponents of the democratic social spirit of our day, who feel the wrongs of the common people and are trying to make the industrial world more just and more fraternal.[45]

An employer of the true social order, will not wrong his employee in order to practice philanthropy afterwards; and a business man of strong Christian character, will work hard to keep his word in business, and deal fairly with laborers and customers. But would not his moral energies be turned in a new direction, if he helped to shape the workings of industry and trade, so that hereafter there will be no fundamental clash between business and the morals of Christianity?[46]

The nation needs leaders who will place the relations of employers and workers in industry, on a basis of justice and goodwill, so that industrial peace can be attained.[47]

In part one of this chapter, has been given a review of conditions in the present economic order as Doctor Rauschenbusch presents them. The subjects considered were, Employer as over against Employee, Work *versus* Wages, and, incidentally, throughout the chapter, Profit *versus* Life.

[44]*The Social Principles of Jesus*, 25.
[45]*The Social Principles of Jesus*, 191.
[46]*Ibid.*, 74.
[47]*Ibid.*, 110.

The problems themselves overlap and blend, hence the discussions have been mostly in the form of concentric circles, the arguments being chiefly concentrated on the unredeemed portion of the social order, since Doctor Rauschenbusch was mainly concerned with the moral elements of the industrial realm of our economic system and its drifts.

The discussions were concerning the business man's attitude toward, and his dealings with, his fellow business men, his employees and the consumers.

Cooperation and an aim toward social unity, based on the principles of solidarity, were suggested as the remedy for the present troubles of the business man.

Also in this chapter were discussed the problems of the laboring-class as viewed from their own standpoint.

Some of the facts pointed out by Doctor Rauschenbusch concerned the physical decline of the morale of the workers, resulting from the deep-rooted injustice of the enormous profits passing to the individuals who have contributed only a fractional part of the creation.

Following is a summary of the chief remedies for these conditions, suggested by Doctor Rauschenbusch, as set forth in this chapter.

If the working class is to rise, its physical fitness must be protected. The industrial wage-earners have the same right of life and health as all others, but to them, vitality and vigor are doubly essential, because the working force of their body and mind, is their whole asset and capital. They need protection against exhausted air and poisonous gases.

A maximum working day and a legal minimum of safety and comfort in the conditions of shop and mine labor, are a concern of civilization and a step toward a Christian social order.

The rise of the working class involves an increase in their share of the profits.

A connected system of employment bureaus, controlled by the class to be served, is needed.

Every laborer should have some technical education.

Public opinion and the law should uphold the working class in their demand for collective bargaining.

The working-class can, by readjustment of political power, secure equal rights in the political field.

Cooperation among laborers as well as among employers, is the way of industrial salvation.

Strong Christian business men are needed who will help shape the workings of industry and trade, in such a way as to establish them upon Christian social principles.

The nation needs, also, leaders who will by legislation, place the relations of employers and employees on a basis of justice and good-will.

"The type of business leadership which took millions out of filthy factory towns, wore out women, and took out the youth from children, cleared twelve percent from slum tenements, kept men and women by high prices and fear of the future—this type of leadership is antiquated."[43]

Extortionate and domineering leadership must be superseded, where the Kingdom of God moves forward.

2

Child Welfare and the Woman Movement

(1) Child Welfare

Doctor Rauschenbusch's moral diagnosis of Business would not be complete without giving his views on these

[43]*The Social Principles of Jesus*, 109. "Personally I am not a despiser of my age and its achievments. The very fact that we can feel our social wrongs so keenly, and discuss them calmly and without fear of social hatred, is one of the highest tributes to be paid to our age. My appeal is made hopefully to the educated reason and the moral insight of modern Christian men."
Christianity and the Social Crisis, 220.

subjects also, since both women and children are factors in the great realm of industrial production and of the economic order.

Affectionate joy in children is perhaps the purest expression of social feeling. Jesus was indignant when the disciples thought children were not of sufficient importance to occupy his attention. To inflict any spiritual injury on one of these little ones, seemed to him an inexpressible guilt. He took them in his arms and blessed them, saying, "Whoever shall not receive the Kingdom of God as a little child, he shall in no wise enter therein."[40]

The child is humanity reduced to its simplest terms and to it also, applies the social principles of the sacredness of life and personality.

Doctor Rauschenbusch relates an incident illustrating the financial rating that a child received in court. In a street accident, on account of crowded traffic, this little one was killed. No damages could be claimed by the parents, because the child had no earning capacity and hence was, economically speaking, worth nothing. So ruled the court. Commenting upon these proceedings, Doctor Rauschenbusch argues that sound and normal children really earn 'their keep' as they are growing up. He claims that a baby is one of the greatest producers of values in in human society, because it stimulates the working capacity of the parents; it is ahead of any contrivance of pleasure, even the piano, the automobile or the phonograph. As a joy-giver it always comes first in rank, no matter what the occasion. In the home, in a social gathering, in the street car, wherever a baby enters, it is the whole center of attraction, and commands attention for a time at least, because it is the highest means of aesthetic pleasure.

The baby developes physical culture for those who care

[40]*Matthew* 18: 1-6; *The Social Principles of Jesus*, 2.

for, and entertain it; by studying the baby, one's knowledge of physiology and psychology is increased. It keeps those with whom it comes in contact, young in spirit, and is a means of character building for those who instruct and train it.

In the study of human nature, the child growing up, furnishes an entire post-graduate course. These are the intellectual, economic and other advantages produced by the child, for its board and clothing, since the true value of any human life cannot be computed in dollars and cents. The little hand of a child, more than the blessing of a priest, consecrates the family."[60]

The child is common property. Not only is it the child of the parents, but it is a child of the community. With no weapon of defense except the cry of pain, it has the right of protection. The rights of a child are based on human solidarity and love. Its rights rise or decline with the prevalent reverence for human life in society, and with the sway of love among us."[61]

At every stage of its life the child belongs to the community and has claims on the community and rights within it. During its earliest period, the family is the community, but as it grows stronger, "its radius of action lengthens and it launches itself on the larger life of the community."[62]

It has a right to father and mother, and to a spacious, clean, wholesome home. If the community has allowed the space around to be crowded and built up with the walls of the houses telescoped, and the light of the rooms obstructed, the child suffers.

The child has a right to grow during all its period of development, but high prices of food will mean short weight boys and girls in the long run. Very many times

[60] Is the Baby Worth a Dollar? *Ladies Home Journal*, XXVII. 19.
[61] Rights of a Child in the Community, *Religious Education*, X, 219.
[62] *Ibid*.

the right to arrive at full stature and vigor has been defeated by premature toil.

The child has also the right to enjoy play. "It has a right to some fun for which it does not have to pay a nickel,"[63] and an inalienable right to keep a pet. How can the boy better get in touch with the soul of the lower creation, than by play with his dog?

A child has a right to an education, and when the mother love is short sighted or stupid, the community must be responsible.

It is the right of a child to have religious instruction, by being introduced to religious stories, to religious books and to God. "Religion is mediated to us by the community of those who have it."[64]

Compared with the selfish ambition of grown-ups, there is something heavenly in children and "they are nearer the Kingdom than those whom the world has smudged."[65] To inflict any spiritual injury on them is ignoring the sacredness of their personality.

The children of the poor who are the product of exploitation, are a standing accusation against society; under-fed, over-stimulated, cut off from clean pleasures of nature, often tainted with vice before knowledge has come, and urged along by the appetites and cruel selfishness of older persons.

France has long been held up as furnishing the terrible example of a declining birth-rate, but the older portions of our country are saved from the same situation only by the fertility of the immigrants. "The chief cause for this profoundly important fact is economic fear."[66] The natives who feel the tightening grip of our industrial

[63]Rights of the Child in the Community, *Religious Education*, X, 225.
[64]*Ibid.*
[65]*The Social Principles of Jesus*, 2.
[66]*Christianity and the Social Crisis*, 278.

development, refuse to bring children into a world which threatens them with poverty.

Cheerful newspaper optimists assure us that the American child makes up by quality what it lacks in numbers. Unfortunately that is merely an effort to make an ugly fact 'look sweet'. "When the reproduction of the race is left to the poor and the ignorant, unusual ability is not transmitted."[57]

Many working mothers go out to labor and the children are left to be educated in the street, which is an educator of doubtful value; and the multitudes of children "who are old enough to work," are forced to help in earning wages.

Play should be the business of these children, yet childhood is denied this recreation on account of the need of the parents and the greed of the employers. It would cut down profit to substitute adult workers. "The killing of play means taking the life out of Life."[58]

The Western Union Telegraph Company hires little boys to deliver its messages, turning their early years into an employment that teaches them nothing for their future career, and often sending them into places of wickedness and crime, to receive their education. "If the mails were under corporation management we should presumably have child letter carriers."[59]

Here is another illustration of the selfishness of employers: "Thirty-one percent of the girls under sixteen employed in the silk weaving industry of Pennsylvania, cost their employers less than two dollars a week."[60]

An additional vase or an extra rug in a wealthy woman's home, may add nothing to the real comfort of any one; yet it may embody the excess toil of a thousand girls for a week. Accepting the social principle of the sacredness of

[57]*Ibid.*, 275.
[58]*Christianizing the Social Order*, 249.
[59]*Ibid.*, 220. [60]*Ibid.*, 244.

life, is it morally tolerable to enjoy excessive luxuries purchased by the excessive toil of others?

"By child labor, the new industries of the present South are using up the manhood and womanhood on which the future South must build its greatness."⁶¹

In the present social order, the children of the rich are perhaps even worse products of exploitation than the poor. "These children, except in conspicuous and fine exceptions, are put out of contact with the people whom they must know if they are to serve them. Besides, the atmosphere of the aristocratic groups feeding but not producing, drugs the sense of obligation, and possesses the mind with the notion that the life and labor of men are made to play tennis with."⁶²

The idle rich, who have vigor of body and mind, and yet produce no useful thing, are to be remembered with pity and compassion. May God forgive them and their children for wasting in refined excess, "what would feed the pale children of the poor, and for taking pride in their workless lives and despising those by whose toil they live." .... "Bless with sevenfold blessing the young lives whose glad growth is being stunted forever, and grant employers of labor, stout hearts to refuse enrichment at such a price. .... Father look with pity upon the children of the streets. Save them from ignorance and brutality, the hardness of greed, the shamelessness of lust and from those that lead Thy children astray. Suffer them to come unto Thee, for Jesus' sake."⁶⁴

(2) The Woman Movement

The attitude of historic Christianity has been a mixture between Jesus' spirit and the spirit of the patriarchal

⁶¹*Christianizing the Social Order*, 276.
⁶²*The Social Principles of Jesus*, 163.
⁶³*Prayers of the Social Awakening*, 89.
⁶⁴*Ibid*, 54.

family. "Today Christianity is plainly prolonging the lines of respect and spiritual valuation, to the point of equality between men and women and beyond."[65]

While the class of working women is slowly making its way through contempt and opposition, there are today many situations where their work is enslaving, and a strangulation of the soul.

The exhausting toil of the one class is the means of piling up the wealth of the other. After the power-machine was invented, it required deftness rather than strength. The slender fingers of women and children sufficed it and their labor was cheaper than that of men, who often saw their own wives wilt and die, under the relentless drag of the machine.[66]

The rapid progress of our country has been due to the wealth of natural resources on the one side, and the physical vigor and mental buoyancy of the human resources on the other side. But today there are large numbers of the wage-earning women who no longer possess this vigor. While the women may be advancing, "they are receding in stamina, and bequeathing an enfeebled equipment to the next generation."[67]

The larger our cities, the wider are the areas from which the perishable food for the working-woman is drawn, and the staler and less nourishing will be the food. Many of the women have been, or are still wives who spend the greater part of their time in the factory. They rarely have had a chance to learn good house-keeping. While the ideal house-wife can make a palatable meal out of almost anything, the tired, wornout factory woman is a poor cook usually.[68] Scorching the steak diminishes its

[65] *The Social Principles of Jesus*, 91.
[66] *Christianity and the Social Crisis*, 217.
[67] *Christianity and the Social Crisis*, 240.
[68] *Ibid.*, 241.

nutritive value, also the appetite of the eater, and both are essential for nutrition.

"Diseases of digestion, fear and anxiety, are the fate of the under-fed and over-worked women, while they are nourishing their children in their pre-natal life."[69]

Our social machinery is almost as blindly cruel as its steel machinery. It runs over the life of a poor worker with scarcely a quiver. Business men feel very differently toward the widow of a business man left in poverty, than they do toward the widow of the poorer classes; these widows are 'cases', while the former, are 'folks'.[70]

Among women, the spirit of the social caste is perhaps more keenly felt than among men, especially the difference in housing, eating, dressing and speaking. The condition of the home often determines the woman. However, in many instances this is not true. There is a strong desire to be like other women, and yet a desire to be different from them.

In Europe, a peasant girl or a servant was quite content with the dress of her class, "but in this country, the instinct of imitation works without a barrier, from the top of the social pyramid to the bottom."[71]

Our industrial system of machinery has absorbed the functions which women formerly fulfilled in the home and has drawn them into the hopper, "because female labor is unorganized cheap labor."

The great majority of girls heartily prefer the independence and the satisfaction of the heart, which are offered to a woman in a comfortable home, but forced to compete with the very men who ought to marry them, they further diminish their own chance of marriage. The optimists speak of it as a sign of progress, that so many professions are now open to woman; the truth of the matter is, that

[69] *Ibid.*, 242.
[70] *Ibid.*, 248.
[71] *Christianity and the Social Crisis*, 268.

it is not choice but grim necessity that drives women into new ways of getting bread and clothing.

Young girls go to work at the very age when their developing bodies ought to be shielded from physical and mental strain. During rush seasons, they are pushed to exhaustion and are kept standing for long hours at a time. Many of them have never learned to keep house well, and poor house-keeping, like poor cooking, is likely to affect the temper and the happiness of the home."

Our capitalistic system deprives the working-class of that leisure and elasticity which would fit them for higher pleasures. On account of poverty, they cannot cultivate and train their aesthetic tastes. These women cannot afford to hear highclass music and plays, or to buy copyrighted books and pictures; hence for them, the "moving picture shows and canned music are the bill of fare."

The monotony of machine work gives no scope for the play of fancy or self-expression. We need a working class with leisure and vitality enough to develop the artistic talent in gifted individuals.

In nearly all industrial sections of the world, the wages of women are too low to support them unaided. "In 1917 only ten percent got more than five hundred dollars a year. Working under a great strain, many a girl at the end of the day is so hysterical and overwrought that her mental balance is plainly disturbed."[14] Too tired for recreation, too tired to read, often too tired to sleep, a girl in financial straits simply yields in a moment of utter weariness and discouragement to the temptations she has withstood up to that moment. A swelling tide of self-pity suddenly overcomes her instincts for decency and righteousness, as

[12]*Christianity and the Social Crisis*, 277.
[13]*Christianizing the Social Order*, 260.
[14]*Ibid.*, 266.

well as the habits for clean living, established by generations of her ancestors.[75]

Thus, to anyone who has learned to think socially and to understand collective forces of society which redeem or ruin thousands, our economic system looms up, like a great collective ravisher of our women.[76]

On account of low wages, a large proportion of working women cannot dress as the requirements of their position and of good taste demand. They cannot afford to keep pace with the frequent changes of fashion.

The fact that the making of women's dress is completely commercialized, accounts for the fashion. They are a succession of arbitrary changes devised by the commercial interests involved, in order to keep women buying.

Of course the changeableness of woman's dress is not wholly due to commercial stimulation. "It is a manifestation of that feminine mutability which has ever been the delight and the despair of men."[77] What enormous amount of time and labor spent on accentuating the charms of women, young and old, with a frame-work of clinging stuffs, of jewels, and of elaborate hair. Men may be more open to the lusts of flesh, but perhaps women make up for it by the lust of the eye and the pride of life. Standards of modesty have changed since women have moved out into freedom. "In matters of dress, men are more modest than women."

"But to many of the best women, the merry-go-round of fashion is a nauseating vertigo."[78] It plunges them into expense, labor and worry; and if left to their own tastes, they would prefer stability. "Does it not concern the Kingdom of God on earth, when an unregenerate economic

[75]*Christianizing the Social Order*, 266; *Christianity and the Social Crisis*, 279.
[76]*Christianizing the Social Order*, 271.
[77]*Ibid.*, 255.
[78]*Christianizing the Social Order*, 255.

system so invades our better life, that good women wear immodest waists and indecent skirts, and trick out their heads with false and unclean things, in order to look like the notorious mistress of a diseased French King?"[79]

"Perhaps it is right that men should instinctively feel that women are morally better than men, but it is a different matter when women think so too."[80] They are not better. They are only good in different ways than men; they have just as much sin and nonsense in them as men have.

Women have pointed out the evils into which masculine mismanagement has brought our social life. But are there no corresponding evils into which the predominant influence of women has already brought us? For example, in domestic service women have always been employers and employees. "This relation is one of the most unsettled and unsatisfactory of all social relations; more feudal and less democratized than any other."[81] The domestic service is unattractive and the worker sits now in an office and allows herself to be sought.

Women handle more money and do it more freely than formerly.[82] Is it accidental, that with the advent of the modern woman, there has been, through all social strata, an increase in the opulence of living, in expensive dress and furniture, in adornments of the table, and in the lavishness of entertainment? These are the things which women control.

However, the Woman Movement is an advancement toward social progress, and its ultimate workings will undoubtedly assist greatly in the promotion of the true social order. "While the movement thrills with splendid

[79]*Ibid.*, 257.
[80]Some Moral Aspects of the Woman Movement, *Biblical World*, XLII, 197.
[81]Some Moral Aspects of the Woman Movement, *Biblical World*, XLII, 105.
[82]*Ibid.*

self-confidence and optimism, half-truths and illusions pertaining to this movement also exist."[83] The results will not be all to the good. The rise of woman will cut some knots, and tie others.

Women have arrived, not only in industry, but also in education and politics. They pervade all domains of life with a sense of equal rights and a feeling of new-found destiny. This is no revolution, but only the beginning of more changes.

"In most educational audiences women predominate. Though they have not generally occupied our pulpits, the men in the pulpits have been conscious of talking to women who could speak their minds,"[84] and who did their own thinking.

"Plainly, they are here as our equals in religion, in intellectual life, in industry, and in the life of our commonwealths."[85] Those who wish success to the movement, must be prepared, however, for the inevitable concomitant evils in it and resist them. Movement into freedom means a severe test of women singly and collectively; a test of a wider field of action, increased liberty, larger duties, untried paths, and unknown passions and temptations.[86]

[83]*Ibid.*, 195-96.
[84]Some Moral Aspects of the Woman Movement, *Biblical World*, XLII, 196.
[85]*Ibid.*, 195. [86]*Ibid.*, 199.

Chapter VIII

MILITARISM, WAR AND CONFLICT WITH EVIL

Since the Great World War has dwarfed and submerged all other issues, including our social problems, and since, in fact, the war and its results present the most acute tremendous social problem of all, in this chapter will be given a review of this subject as Doctor Rauschenbusch has discussed it in several of his books.

During the strenuous years of the World War, while many had reason to query as to what had become of the democratic faith, social consciousness and passion for liberty, that Doctor Rauschenbusch had claimed, he was writing his last book, "A Theology for the Social Gospel." In this book are clear and definite statements, which dispel entirely any doubt as to his attitude toward militarism and war.

His long silence on the motive and aims of the Allies, and his failure to protest against the Germans, awakened doubts and bewilderment in the minds of some of his friends and readers, to whom he had interpreted the social gospel.

Following is a quotation, and later on, are statements by him, which perhaps express in part, his feelings for the Fatherland, without in the least casting any reflections upon himself as a true and loyal American citizen. "It has been Germany's unhappy fate to formulate as a doctrine which other nations practice under temptation, and to be the champion of two hateful remnants of the past—autocracy and war."[1]

Because life seems to consist of money and the problems of pursuing gain, wars are begun for its support. War is

[1]Taylor, Graham, Walter Rauschenbusch, *Survey*, XL, 493.

a rupture of fellowship on a large scale, and the most extensive demonstration of the collapse of love, which any person has ever seen.

The ultimate cause of this World War was that same lust for easy and unearned gain, discussed in the previous chapters. This lust has created those internal evils under which every nation has suffered intensely.

According to Jesus, human life and personality are sacred. Wars and prostitution are the most flagrant offences against this social principle. "War is a wholesale waster of life and prostitution is the worst form of contempt for personality."[1]

The demand for disarmament and permanent peace, for the rights of small nations against imperialistic and colonizing powers, for freedom of the seas and of trade routes, and for orderly settlement of grievances; these are demands for social righteousness and fraternity on a large scale.

Our nation armed itself to invade another country for the purpose of overthrowing the German Government, and on the ground that the existence of autocratic governments are a menace to the peace of the world.

The momentous declaration of President Wilson, recognized the fact that the governments of Great States may in reality be only groups of men using their fellowmen as pawns, and that such governments have in the past waged war for dynastic and class interests without consulting the people. While "there is no doubt that these charges justly characterize the German government, there is also no doubt that they characterize all governments of past history with few exceptions, and that even the democratic governments of today, are not able to show clean hands on these points."[2]

[1] *The Social Principles of Jesus*, 12.
[2] *A Theology for the Social Gospel*, 74, 75.

The social gospel has succeeded in awakening the conscience of this nation and we are grateful for the leader of our country who wants peace. "The President deserves our earnest support in standing for the noble ends to which he has given such remarkable expressions."[4]

"The Great War is a catastrophic stage in the Kingdom of God and its direct effects will operate for generations."[5]

While before the War, the social gospel dealt with social classes, today it is being expanded into international terms. The problem of international peace is the problem of expanding love and social unity. "It is the social sin of Christendom, that so few took the problem seriously until we were chastised for our moral stupidity."[6]

This problem of peace will continue to be one for the intellect and the conscience of our young men and women of today, and it will take a life-time or more to see it through.[7] But in the meantime, it is our duty to see that no innocent blood is wasted. Our chief interest should be the desire for a social order in which the work and the freedom of every least human being, will be honored and protected. We should have an attitude of conscientious objection toward the coercive and militaristic governments.

The Great War has forced us to realize the enormous tasks of international relations, such as the prevention of armed conflicts, the elimination of the irritant causes of war, the protection of small nations which possess what the big nations covet, and the creation of an institutional basis for a great family of nations in days to come.

[4] *Survey*, XL, 494.
[5] *A Theology for the Social Gospel*, 226.
[6] "Having a son who with my approval is at the front to help in meeting the present offensive, ...we best realize some things through our children;" Taylor, Graham; Walter Rauschenbusch, *Survey*, XL, 495.
[7] *The Social Principles of Jesus*, 26.

"Where militarism rules, war is idealized by monuments, paintings, poetry and song. The stench of the hospitals and the maggots of the battle-field are passed in silence, and the imagination of the people is filled with waving plumes and the shout of charging columns."[8]

Very few wars have ever been fought for the sake of justice or for the people, and if war is ever to be relegated to the past ages of outgrown barbarism, we must shake off its magic.[9]

That impression of undeserved mass misery, which the war has brought home to the thoughtless, has long been weighing on the minds of those who understood the social principles of Jesus.

The war has deeply affected the religious assurance of our own time, and will lessen it still more when the excitement is over and the aftermath of innocent suffering becomes clear. This fact confronts us, that war is certainly contagious. One nation arms because it fears another; the other arms more because this armament alarms it. "Each subsidizes a third and fourth to aid; and a planet is stained red in a solidarity of hate and horror."[10]

But all whose Christianity has not been thrown aside by the catastrophe, are demanding a Christianizing of international relations.

"When war inflames a nation, it is faith to believe that a peaceable disposition is a workable inter-national policy."[11] Amidst the disunion of almost entire Christendom, it is faith to look for unity and to express unity in action. It is faith to see God at work in the world and to claim a share in the same task.

The Great War was in truth a grim discussion of the

[8] *Christianity and the Social Crisis*, 350.
[9] *Ibid*.
[10] *A Theology for the Social Gospel*, 80.
[11] *A Theology for the Social Gospel*, 102.

future of the race on this planet, but a discussion with
both reason and religion left out. The sufferings of a
single righteous man deeply moved the psalmist or the
poet of Job, but in this age, entire social classes challenged
the justice of the God who afflicted them by permitting
this wicked social system. It revolts them to see these
unjust sufferings and miseries perpetuated by law and
organized force, or justified by the makers of public
opinion. Where these people see blind force working
dumb agony, we must see moral will working toward
redemption and education."

One of the universal sins of organized society which co-
operated in the death of Christ was militarism. Though
Jesus probably never passed through an actual war, nor
was he likely ever forced to bear arms; yet that he had
convictions on war is plain from his sayings. "He that
taketh the sword shall perish by the sword." He compre-
hended the fact that in war neither side gains and that
the reactions of war are as dangerous as the direct
effects."

When Jesus was arrested he fell into the hands of the
war system. When his back was beaten with the leaded
whip, when the crown of thorns was pressed into his scalp,
when he was draped in the purple mantle and saluted as
the 'King of the Jews,' he experienced the humor of the
barrack-room. This was sport for the professional
soldiers of the Roman Empire. The men who drove the
nails through his hands and feet were the equivalent of a
firing squad at an excution; and when they gambled for
his clothes, they were taking their soldiers' perquisites.

When we call out the militant spirit even in religion, we
summon a dangerous power. It has always bred grim-

[12] *Ibid.*, 223.
[13] *A Theology for the Social Gospel*, 223.

ness and cruelty. Crusaders and inquisitors did work in the name of Jesus but not in his spirit.[14]

Hate breeds hate, force challenges force. "Only forgiveness kills an enemy and leaves a friend."[15] "Jesus blended virility with gentleness and wherever his followers used force to defend him, the Kingdom of Heaven has dropped to the level of brutal empires. Though he resisted and fought even on the cross, it was not with brutal weapons."[16] He resisted by the quietness which both maddens and disarms. The most striking thing in his bearing is his silence; however, "he never yielded an inch and he was in perfect command of the situation."[17]

"The Kingdom of God can never be promoted by lies, craft, crime or war," though there will be constant conflict with evil as long as the Kingdom of Evil exists.[18]

The Great World War was the result of public and organized evil, as much a conflict with powers as with earthly magistrates. Even today the future is heavily clouded and uncertain, but "our faith still holds that even the great disaster will help ultimately to weaken the despotic and exploiting forces, and make the condition of the common people more than ever the chief concern of science and statesmanship."[19]

If the World War leads to the downfall or regeneration of all governments which support the exploitation of the masses by powerful groups, it will have been worth its cost;[20] if the nations emerge into a long peace with disarmament, this war will be recorded as a holy and redemptive war. "Not he who kills and subjugates, but he who

[14]*The Social Principles of Jesus*, 157.
[15]*Ibid.*
[16]*A Theology for the Social Gospel*, 263.
[17]*A Theology for the Social Gospel*, 263.
[18]*Ibid.*, 135.
[19]*The Social Principles of Jesus*, 43.
[20]*A Theology for the Social Gospel*, 75.

Militarism, War and Conflict With Evil 99

makes life safe and happy shall have the statue set up in his honor."[21]

Jesus accepted the kingship but repudiated force. To his mind the absence of force-resistance was characteristic of his whole undertaking. He believed in power based on spiritual coherence. His great social problem was redemption from evil. Every step of approach toward the Kingdom of God must be won by a struggle which means constructive conflict of a high order.[22]

When governments and political oligarchies in monarchies and in semi-democracies, submit to real Christian democracy, "they step out of the Kingdom of Evil into the Kingdom of God."[23] "The conflict between the Christian and unChristian forces in our social order is a real war, but it is a conflict of principalities and powers in high places."[24] God is for the Kingdom of God, and his Kingdom does not mean injustice and the perpetuation of innocent suffering.

"O Lord, grant to the rulers of nations, faith in the possibility of peace through justice...... Bless our soldiers and sailors for their swift obedience and their willingness to answer to the call of duty, but inspire them none the less with a hatred of war...... Teach our age nobler methods of matching our strength and more effective ways of giving our life for the flag..... O Thou strong Father of all nations, grant that peace may come on earth at last, and that Thy sun may shed its light rejoicing on a holy brotherhood of peoples."[25]

In this chapter has been pointed out Doctor Rauschenbusch's tender feelings for the people of Germany and at

[21]*The Social Principles of Jesus*, 108.
[22]*A Theology for the Social Gospel*, 117.
[23]*Ibid.*
[24]*Christianizing the Social Order*, 241.
[25]*Prayers of the Social Awakening*, 97, 98.

the same time his hatred toward autocracy and war; his loyalty for America, his genuine support of President Wilson's aim toward international peace and the following statements against the militaristic system as well as his general discussions on war:

The cause of war is lust for unearned gain. It is a waster of life and a flagrant offence against the social principles of Jesus.

The demands for peace and disarmament, for the rights of small nations against imperialistic power, and for social unity, are the demands for social righteousness.

The problem of international peace is the problem of expanding love and fraternity, and this problem will continue throughout generations to come.

The Great World War has compelled us to realize the greatness and urgency of the task of adjusting international relations and of protecting the small nations which possess what the powerful nations covet.

We must shake off the magic of war if we wish to relegate war to the past ages of barbarism.

The Great War has deeply affected the religious assurance of our time, on account of the mass-suffering of the innocent.

All sincere and faithful Christians demand a Christianizing of international relations.

It is faith to see God's hand in the world and to claim a share in the same task of Christianizing the social order.

Militarism was one of the universal sins of organized society which compassed the death of Christ.

Crusaders and inquisitors did their work in the name of Jesus, but not in his spirit.

Jesus resisted but not with brutal weapons, and yet he had perfect command of the situation at his death.

If this World War leads to the downfall of autocracy

and the nations emerge into permanent peace with disarmament and equal rights, it will be worth its cost.

The conflict between the Christian and unChristian forces in our social order is a conflict between principalities and powers in high places.

The Kingdom of God and the King do not stand for injustice and inhuman suffering. There is a nobler method of matching our strength than by war, and there are more effective ways of giving our life for the flag.

We must hope and pray for international peace and a holy brotherhood of peoples.

Real democracy will be the result of conquest—a step out of the Kingdom of Evil into the Kingdom of God.

Chapter IX

THE CHURCH AS A SOCIAL FACTOR OF SALVATION

Since in the previous chapters the workings of the Kingdom of Evil have been pointed out in the various modern social problems as discussed by Doctor Rauschenbusch, and since in the past, the Church has been the organized opposing force in the conflict, it is the purpose of this chapter to consider the Church as a social factor of the salvation of society. The discussions will be as set forth in Doctor Rauschenbusch's major books, and are mainly concerning the influence of the Church in the past, its faults and mistakes, and its presnt opportunity.

(1) Its Influence in the Past

When Jesus said, "Ye are the salt of the earth," and, "ye are the light of the world," he was addressing the charter members of the Church Universal—the beginning of organized Christianity.

The Christian Church began its history as a community of inspiration. By 'the Church' is meant, of course, the great body of Christian believers, or Christianity in general.

"The Church which Jesus organized, grew out of his social feeling for the sufferings of the common people, and from his aim to straighten out the affairs of the world so that the wrongs of the righteous would be redressed.[1] Since that time Christianity has been a power in the land to cleanse and to fraternalize the social life, and as long as the Churches were well led, they were able to control the moral life of entire communities.

[1] *The Social Principles of Jesus*, 69.

It has been said that the creation of the Church was the most important event in the history of Christianity. By the Church, has the memory of Jesus' life and the consciousness of salvation been transmitted to us. This consciousness we obtain by sharing the common faith and experience of the Church. An individual is by nature subject to moral burdens which often overwhelm him and from which, if unaided, he cannot escape. Help must come to him from some source above his own level. If the Church makes and recognizes Jesus as its initiator, and Christ as the central idea of Christianity, then the individual can receive his help and relief through the Church.[2] This help comes to him by the consciousness of solidarity which is one of the fundamental principles of religion. The saving power of the Church rests on the presence of the Kingdom of God within it.[3]

The Church offers to Christ not only many human bodies and minds to serve as ministers of his salvation, but its own composite personality. It offers to us, a collective memory stored with great hymns and Bible stories, and deeds of heroism with trained aesthetic and moral feeling, and with a collective will set on righteousness[4]

When it is organized around Christ as its impelling power, it brings social forces to bear on evil and to establish much good. During the formative years of our own national growth, the Churches gathered up available resources of education, history, philosophy, eloquence, art and music, and established social centers with higher motives than mere family, money, gossip, the daily paper, and the inevitable vices.[5]

We are so accustomed to the Churches, that we hardly

[2] *A Theology for the Social Gospel*, 127.
[3] *Ibid.*, 130.
[4] *A Theology for the Social Gospel*, 119.
[5] *Ibid.*, 121.

realize what a social force they have been, and what influence they have exerted over the minds of the community. In many instances the Church has given health to the bodies and calmness and self-control to the minds, by subduing their souls with a positive faith.⁶

It has been pointed out in a previous chapter that one of the most important characteristics of religion is, that it constitutes a bond of social groups. Therefore it is the business of preachers and the leaders of the Church, by their teaching and by the influence of their lives, to produce "the characteristic of love and fraternity in Christian men and women."⁷ Without the consciousness of solidarity, religion can neither be rightly understood nor rightly lived.

If there had never been such an organization as the Christian Church, every great religious mind would dream of the possibility of creating something like it. He would see the possibility of its power of reaching out by free loyalty springs of action and character lying too deep for civil law and even for education to stir. "He might well imagine, too, how the presence of such a social group would quicken and balance the civil and the political community."⁸

Thorough salvation changes a man so that he turns from self to God and humanity.

"Any religious experience in which our fellowmen have no part or thought, does not seem to be a distinctively Christian experience."⁹ Therefore since the Church propagates and perpetuates the religious life, its vitality is of importance to the higher life of humanity. It must have the law and spirit of Jesus.

The Kingdom ideal is the test and corrective of the in-

⁶*Ibid.*, 12.
⁷*A Theology for the Social Gospel*, 273.
⁸*Ibid.*, 120.
⁹*Ibid.*, 97.

fluence of the Church; and since the Kingdom is the chief end of God, it must be the purpose for which the Church stands.[10]

In America the Christian Church is actually deeply affected by sympathy with the social movement. It believes heartily in political democracy, and therefore can easily learn to believe in industrial democracy, as soon as it comprehends the connection.[11] American ministers naturally take a keen interest in public life, and as well as they know how, have tried to bring the religious forces to bear at least on some aspects of public affairs.

"Liquor's authority has been overcome by the Church, apparently at least, before either business or science lent much aid."[12]

The modern movement of foreign missions was the response of the spirit of Christ in the Church to the opportunity presented by the new world-wide commerce. With all the faults that anyone can point out in it, the foreign mission work of the modern Church is one of the most splendid expressions of the Christ spirit in history; full of blessing for the Church at home, and fuller of historic importance for the future of mankind than any man can now foresee.[13]

The authority of the group over the individual within it, and its power to impose its own moral standard on its membership by virtue of which it educates them upward, if its standard is high, counts for much through its influence in the general social life.

"The Church is a social institution along the side of the family, the industrial organization of society, and the State. The Kingdom of God is in all of these and realizes itself through them all."[14] It is indispensable to

[10]*Ibid.*, 143.
[11]*Christianity and the Social Crisis*, 323.
[12]*A Theology for the Social Gospel*, 64.
[13]*Christianity and the Social Crisis*, 318.
[14]*A Theology for the Social Gospel*, 145.

the religious education of humanity and to the conservation of religion; and the greatest future awaits religion in the public life of humanity.

This is the noblest view we can take of the Church, that the Spirit of the Lord has always been an informing principle of life within her, and that "though faltering, sinning, and defiled, she has kept her own collective personality intact."[15]

The power of leadership is with those organizations and movements which have some prophetic qualities and trust to the inner light. Primitive Christian communities were prophetic and they stood for social righteousness. They were against war, against capital punishment, against slavery and against coercion in matters of religion.[16] Today great Church bodies stand, as a matter of course, on these principles of freedom and toleration which only the boldest once dared to assert.[17]

The rise of social Christianity is felt in all the institutional agencies of the American Churches. The Young Men's Christian Association has developed a splendid machinery for constructive social service. The Young Women's Christian Association in 1911 definitely committed itself to the business of securing a living wage and a maximum working day for women workers.

The Student Volunteer Movement and the Layman's Missionary Movement have been compelled to lay stress on the social conception of missions. The Men and Religion Forward Movement of 1911 is another evidence of the ascendency of social Christianity.

Though the awakening of the Church is far from complete, these movements have proven that the present generation in the nation and in the Church, will not be satisfied with any kind of Christianity that does not un-

[15]*Ibid.*, 70.
[16]*Ibid.*, 106.
[17]*A Theology for the Social Gospel*, 106.

dertake to Christianize the social order.[18] The Church must embody Christ, and live according to the social principles of Jesus, if it is to have saving power. It must translate the personal life of Jesus Christ into the social life of its group and thus bring it to bear on the individual.

In 1906 a number of the Protestant Church bodies were on the point of entering into organic union whose proposed creed contained an article in which was stated their belief that men of the Christian faith exist for the service of men, not only in holding forth the word of life, but in the support of works and institutions of pity and charity, in the maintenance of human freedom, in the deliverance of all those that are oppressed, in the enforcement of civic justice, and in the rebuke of all unrighteousness.[19]

The Brotherhood of the Kingdom, formed in 1893, was one of the earliest organizations of social Christianity in the country.

One of the most important practical questions is the attitude of the Roman Catholic Church to the social movements. It exerts a far stronger control over the social affiliations and the ideas of its members, than the Protestant Churches. Many of its priests live with and for the poor and are splendid incarnations of personal democracy.[20]

For years to come, this new social interest in the Church will be vague, groping, sentimental, timid and inefficient. We shall be like an army moving against a hillside before the enemy's batteries are unmasked. Nevertheless, the Church is moving on.[21]

[18]*Christianizing the Social Order*, 18, 19.
[19]*Christianizing the Social Order*, 21.
[20]*Ibid.*, 26.
[21]*Ibid.*, 29.

(2) Its Faults and Mistakes of the Past

The men who stand for the social gospel, have been among the most active critics of the Church, because they have realized most clearly both the great needs of our social life, and the potential capacities of the Church to meet them. Hence "their criticism has been a form of compliment to the Church."[22]

If Christianity set out with a great social ideal, and has made mistakes in the past, in order to advance, it is necessary to recognize these shortcomings, so the questions are asked, "What are the criticisms?" and "Why are the failures?"

The 'long eclipse' of the social ideal was due to various causes. One of the chief of these was that the Kingdom Ideal had not remained at the altitude to which Jesus had lifted it, but had relapsed into the crudeness of pre-Christian apocalypticism."[23]

The other-worldly hope gained ascendency and the hope of heaven absorbed the religious fervor which might have reached out for a better life on earth. Also, the Church which was founded on democracy and brotherhood, had in its higher levels become an organization controlled by the upper classes for parasitic ends— a religious duplicate of the coercive State, and a chief check on the advance of democracy and brotherhood. The decline of democracy within the Church, weakened the religious force of democratic and social aspirations, and speculative theology crowded out the social ideas.[24]

The Church was greatly influenced by tradition and dogma. Popular superstition, inculcated by the teaching authority built up an overwhelming impression of the

[22] *A Theology for the Social Gospel*, 121.
[23] *Christianizing the Social Order*, 71.
[24] *Christianizing the Social Order*, 73.

power of evil, and the Christian spirit was thrown into an attitude of defense only.

Superstitions which originated in the third century are still faithfully cultivated by great churches, compressing the minds of the young with fear and cherished by the old, as their most precious faith.[25]

Religious bigotry, the combination of graft and political power, the corruption of justice, the mob spirit, militarism and class contempt, are all forces of the Kingdom of Evil which have corrupted the Church. "Religious bigotry has been one of the permanent evils of mankind, the cause of untold social division and bitterness."[26] It takes religion to put a steel edge on social intolerance. Just because it is so high and its command of social loyalty so great, it is pitiless when it goes wrong. It was ecclesiastical religion that killed Jesus.[27]

It is the duty of the Church to bring love, unity and freedom to mankind; instead, it created division, fomented hatred and stifled social liberty. Theoretically the Church is the great organization of unselfish service. Actually, it has been profoundly concerned for its own power and authority.

Protestantism was thrust by violent reactions of the Reformation into exaggerated individualism, but all who have had to acquire a social and historical comprehension laboriously, will appreciate how little the old Protestant system stimulated and developed the understanding of the social factor in redemption.

The dogmas and theological ideas of the early Church were those ideas which at that time were needed to hold the Church together, to rally its forces, but today many of those ideas are without present significance.[28] Hence

[25] *A Theology for the Social Gospel*, 79.
[26] *Ibid.*, 249.
[27] *Ibid.*, 250.
[28] *A Theology for the Social Gospel*, 13.

the world is full of stale religion. Theology bears part of the guilt for the pride, the greed and the ambition of the church.[29] In some of the problems of theology, even the terminology is difficult for anyone to understand unless he has lived under Church influence for years. Jesus spoke in the language of the laymen who were his followers. "The renovating effect of the social gospel would aid theology to meet the really modern religious needs."[30]

True social insight knows that the sins of the Church were always the sins of the age. While the Church influences society, society has always influenced the church, and when it has dropped to the level of its environment, it has simply yielded to the law of social gravitation.

"If society continues to disintegrate and decay, the Church will be carried down with it."[31]

Today the sins of the Church are mainly sins of omission; yet the contrast between the force of good which it might exert, and the force which it does exert in public life, produces profounder feelings than the shortcomings of the State.

Much of the religion of the Church is still mainly individualistic, "which religion has bred saints, missionaries, pastors and scholars, but few prophets."[32]

God made us for one another and our highest perfection comes not by isolation, but by love and fraternity. The way of holiness comes through human fellowship and service. "Prophecy springs up where fervent religious experience combines with a democratic spirit, strong social feeling and free utterance."[33]

It is also the business of the Church to encourage, tem-

[29]*Ibid.*, 135.
[30]*Ibid.*, 17.
[31]*Chrstianity and the Social Crisis*, 341.
[32]*A Theology for the Social Gospel*, 194.
[33]*Ibid.*

per and purify the intellectual, as well as the emotional and volitional experiences of its members.

The delinquencies of the Church lie heavily on our minds when we hold up the Church as the great organism of salvation. If we are to judge it by its own absolute criteria as the body of Christ and the exponent of his spirit, the gap between the ideal and the reality is painful. The fact is, that the Church "has watered its own stock and cannot pay dividends on all the paper it has issued. It has made claims for itself which no organization composed of human lives can live up to."[34]

Every community is inclined to develop an expanded self-consciousness if the opportunity is at all favorable and the Christian Church has certainly not let its opportunity go by.[35]

It is important to remember that when its high claims were first developed, they were largely true. Christianity was in sharp opposition not only to the State, but to the whole social life surrounding it. Christian influences were not yet diffused in society and literature, so "there was actually no salvation outside of the Church."[36]

Even today many Christians cannot see any religious importance in social justice and fraternity, because it does not increase the number of conversions nor fill the churches. "Secular life is belittled as compared with Church life," and services rendered to the Church receive a higher religious rating than services rendered to the community.[37]

Every forward step in the historical evolution of religion, has been marked by a closer union of religion and ethics and by the elimination of non-ethical religious

[34] *A Theology for the Social Gospel*, 122.
[35] *Ibid.*, 118.
[36] *Ibid.*
[37] *Ibid.*, 186.

performances. This union of ethics and religion reached its highest perfection in the life and mind of Jesus.[38]

Wherever the Church has lost the saving influence of Christ, it has lost its saltness and is a tasteless historical survival. It is historically self-evident that church bodies do lose the saving power, and if Christ is not in the Church, how does it differ from the world?[39]

Religion may develop an elaborate system of its own, wheels within wheels, and instead of being a dynamic of righteousness in the natural social relations of men, its energies may be consumed in driving its own machinery. "Instead of being the power-house supplying the Kingdom of God among men with power and light, the Church may exist for its own sake,"[40] becoming an expensive consumer of wealth, a conservative clog and a real hinrance of social progress.

"Any person who has failed to adjust his religion to his growing powers and his intellectual horizon, has failed in one of the most important functions of growth, just as if his cranium failed to expand and to give room to his brain."[41]

Religion must be geared to the big live issues of today, if it is to manifest its full saving energies. The Church's inspiring teaching must meet the new social problems so effectively that evil cannot last or grow beyond remedy.[42]

An enlightened conscience cannot help feeling a growing sense of responsibility and guilt for the common sins under which humanity is bound, and to which we all contribute.

"The Church has quenched the spirit; it has discountenanced prophesyings; it has forbidden intellectual scru-

[38] *A Theology for the Social Gospel*, 14.
[39] *Ibid.*, 128.
[40] *The Social Principles of Jesus*, 141.
[41] *Ibid.*, 142.
[42] *The Social Principles of Jesus*, 143.

tiny of inspiration, so far as the biblical books were concerned."

It has killed the spirit of the law by keeping the letter of it. "The social gospel scorns the tithing of mint, anise and cummin, at which the Pharisees are still busy, and it insists on getting down to the weightier matters of God's law, to justice and mercy."⁴⁴

No social group or organization, which drains others for its own ease, and resists the effort to abate this fundamental evil, can claim to be clearly within the Kingdom of God.⁴⁵

The Church needs to carry forward in patience the eternal cross of Christ, counting it for joy if sown as grains of wheat in the furrows of the world, for only by the agony of the righteous comes redemption. Any advance of social righteousness is seen as a part of redemption and arouses inward joy.⁴⁶

"A fresh understanding for the indispensableness of the Church is gaining ground today in spite of the increased knowledge of its past and present failures."⁴⁷ Nothing lasts unless it is organized, and if it is organized of human life, we must put up with the qualities of human life in it. Our sins and shortcomings are due to the feebleness with which we realize God.

(3) Its Present Opportunity

Since the Kingdom is the supreme end of God, it must be the purpose for which the Church stands, and the measure in which it fulfills this purpose is the measure of its spiritual authority and honor. Our Christianity is most Christian, when religion and ethics are viewed as in-

⁴³*A Theology for the Social Gospel*, 91.
⁴⁴*Ibid.*, 192.
⁴⁵*Ibid.*, 15.
⁴⁶*Prayers of the Social Awakening*, 118.
⁴⁷*A Theology for the Social Gospel*, 123.

separable elements of the same single-minded and wholehearted life, in which the consciousness of God and the consciousness of Humanity blend completely.[48]

It has been pointed out that the crisis of society is also the crisis of the Church, and that it cannot thrive when society continues to decay. But, on the other hand, the present crisis of society presents one of the greatest opportunities for the growth and development of the Church, that have ever been offered to Christianity.[49]

In all of the greatest forward movements of humanity, religion has been one of the driving forces. If Christianity would add its moral force to the social and economic forces making for a nobler organization of society, "it could render such help to the cause of justice and righteousness, as would make this a proud page in the history of the Church."[50]

The social gospel is God's predestined agent to continue what the Reformation began. The Church must either condemn the world and seek to change it, or tolerate it and conform to it.

But it is futile to attempt to reform modern society on biblical models. It is true that any regeneration of society must come only through the act of God and the presence of Christ, but God is now acting, and Christ is now here. We must have the faith of the apostolic Church plus the knowledge which nineteen centuries of history have given us.[51]

The social gospel is a union of religion and ethics and is likely to be a wholesome Christianizing force in Christian thought. It plainly concentrates religious interest on the great ethical problems of social life.

The social gospel is a permanent addition to our spirit-

[48]*Ibid.*, 14.
[49]*Christianity and the Social Crisis*, 332.
[50]*Christianity and the Social Crisis*, 336.
[51]*Ibid.*, 346.

ual outlook. It is not only already being preached, but it has already set new problems for local church-work, and has turned the pastoral and organizing work of the ministry into new constructive directions.[52] Its interests not only lie on earth within the relations of the life that now is, but it is practical in the teachings of the life to come.[53] It is possible to preach both an individualistic and a social gospel with full effectiveness.

"It would strengthen the appeal of the social gospel if evil could be regarded as a variable factor in the life of humanity, which it is our duty to diminish for every young life and for every new generation."[54]

As to individualistic religion, it is right to believe in prayer and meditation in the presence of God, in the conscious purging of the soul from fear, love of gain and selfish ambition, through realizing God, in bringing the intellect into alignment with the mind of Christ. "When a man goes up against hard work, conflict, loneliness and the cross, it is right to lean back on the Eternal and draw from the silent reservoirs. But what we receive thus, is for use,"[55] for the promotion of the Kingdom of God, and for establishing a true social order.

The social gospel furnishes new tests for religious experiences. "We are not disposed to accept the converted souls whom the individualistic evangelism supplies without looking them over."[56] To one whose memories run back to Moody's time, the methods now used by some evangelists seem calculated to produce only 'skin-deep changes.' Things have simmered down to signing a card, shaking hands with, or being introduced to the evangelist,"[57] and salvation is thus received. Some who have been 'saved'

[52] *A Theology for the Social Gospel*, 2.
[53] *Ibid.*, 42.
[54] *Ibid.*, 33.
[55] *Ibid.*, 7.
[56] *A Theology for the Social Gospel*, 96.
[57] *Ibid.*, 97.

and perhaps consecrated a number of times, are worth no more to the Kingdom of God than they were before. Some become worse through their 'revival experiences,' more self-righteous, more opinionated, more steeped in unrealities, and stupid over against the most important things, more devoted to emotions, and unresponsive to real duties.[58]

It is time to over-haul our understanding of the kind of change we hope to produce by personal conversion and regeneration.

Theology is not superior to the gospel, it merely exists to the aid in the preaching of salvation. Individualistic theology has not given us an adequate understanding of the sinfulness of the social order and its share in the sins of all individuals within it. Neither has it evoked faith in the will and power of God to redeem the permanent institutions of human society from their inherited guilt of oppression and extortion. The teachings of the social gospel aim to bring men under repentance for their collective sins and to create a more sensitive and more modern conscience for society.[59]

The social gospel is believed by trinitarians and unitarians alike, by Catholic Modernists and Kansas Presbyterians of the strictest order. "Though not always arousing loyalty to the Church, it arouses a fresh, warm loyalty to Christ wherever it goes."[60] All who believe in it are at one in desiring the spiritual sovereignty of Christ in humanity.

The American churches are a part of the American nation, an organization of the people, by the people and for the people. But even outside the churches, the social awakening is remarkable for the religious spirit it creates

[58] *Ibid.*, 96.
[59] *A Theology for the Social Gospel*, 5.
[60] *Ibid.*, 148.

Church as a Social Factor of Salvation 117

in men who thought "they were done with religion."[61] Among many Americans it has become a constructive force in politics.

The new social problems must further be met by the inspiring teaching of the Church, so effectively, that the social awakening will become general.

Among the many modern problems and not the least to be considered, is the redemption of our penal system. Our prisons are still human hells, where men are cut off from all that exercises a saving influence on our lives—the love of wife and child and home, work or play, contact with nature, hope, ambition—only fear and coercion are in full force.[62]

Here too, the Church must use her influence to revolutionize the whole system.

The chief interest of the Church in any millenium is the desire for a social order in which the worth and freedom of every being will be protected, whether in prison or out.

"O Master, give us thine inflexible sternness against sin, and thine inexhaustible compassion for the frailty and tragedy of those who do sin."[63]

"If the future life is to be the consummation of all that is good and divine here, it must offer fellowship with God and with man. This is the point to be insisted on in our popular teaching, and not the painlessness and the eternal rest."[64]

The Church as such, has been through its insistence upon a creedal interpretation of the teachings of Christ, at times the greatest enemy of the true social gospel.

Christianity has been in the main taken by professed

[61]*Christianizing the Social Order*, 7.
[62]*A Theology for the Social Gospel*, 214.
[63]*Prayers of the Social Awakening*, 82.
[64]*A Theology for the Social Gospel*, 236.

Christians as a theological and metaphysical doctrine rather than as a practical, ethical and social attitude.

Another obstacle to the social success of Christianity, has been the failure of its representatives to appreciate the importance of material and economic factors in the life of man. Man is not only a spiritual, but also a material being hemmed in by the forces of the material world. The social failure of historical Christianity in the past has been largely due to the non-recognition of this truth and this is one of the main reasons why some men have lost their faith in the social power of religion.

The success of individuals, of churches, of communities, and of nations, depends on integrity, faith, industry, brotherly kindness and an interest in the body of man as well as the soul.

When the Kingdom of God is at stake, a man saves his life by losing it, and loses his life by saving it, and the loss of his higher self cannot be offset by any amount of external gain.[65]

Social redemption is brought by vicarious suffering, so, bearing the cross became another social principle of Jesus. He saw the cross on the horizon of his life long before others saw it.

The cross of Christ contributes to strengthen the power of prophetic religion and therewith the redemptive forces of the Kingdom of God.

The era of prophetic and democratic Christianity has just begun, yet "social Christianity is by all tokens the great highway by which this present generation can come to God.[66] It is a fusion between the new understanding created by the social sciences and the teachings and moral ideals of Christianity. If Christianity is henceforth to discharge its full energy in the regeneration of social life, it especially needs the allegiance of college men and women

[65]*The Social Principles of Jesus*, 173.
[66]*Christianizing the Social Order*, 118.

Church as a Social Factor of Salvation 119

who have learned to understand to some degree, the facts and laws of human society.[67]

If the ideals of social Christianity can win the active minds of the present generation of college students, it will swing a part of the enormous organized forces of the Christian Church to bear on the social tasks of our American communities, and that will help to create the nobler American which we see by faith.[68]

"We need the ancient spirit of prophecy and the leaping fire and the joy of a new conviction, and dauntless courage to face the vast needs of the future."[69]

But it is encouraging to realize that the Church is moving on and the Master of the Church is behind it. "He has sounded forth the trumpet that shall never blow retreat."[70]

The purpose of this chapter has been to present the situation of the Church, its past failures, its successes, its present task and its future outlook. The main concern in these discussions is, what is the Church to do, and how shall it be done?

The appeal by Doctor Rauschenbusch as to how the Church may be a factor in the salvation of the social order, is hopefully made to the educated reason and the moral insight of modern Christian men.

The presentation and practical application of the social gospel is the method strongly advocated as the effective remedy for conditions of the present crisis in society.

The Church was claimed by Jesus to be the light of the world. In spite of its mistakes and failures it has been an organized force against evil and has stood for

[67]*The Social Principles of Jesus*, 196.
[68]*Prayers of the Social Awakening*, 82.
[69]*The Social Principles of Jesus*, 196.
[70]*Christianizing the Social Order*, 29.

righteousness. It propagates and perpetuates the religious life and brings vitality to the higher life of humanity.

The Church has been a saving influence in society, but society has also influenced the Church. The decline of democracy in the Church weakened the religious force and it became corrupted. Selfishness, greed and graft within, caused the power for good to decline.

Its religion was largely individualistic, and the Christian set his hopes mainly on the future world. Personal santification must serve the Kingdom of God. A religious experience is not Christian unless it binds us closer to men and commits us more deeply to the Kingdom. It has been said that, other things being equal, a solidaristic religious experience is more distinctively Christian.

The social gospel is the old message of salvation, but it has been enlarged and intensified. It is built on the foundation of the apostles and prophets.

If the church is to be progressive, it must allow and aid religion to adjust itself to modern times."[11] The sense of solidarity is one of the true marks of the followers of Jesus.

It has been also shown that if the Kingdom of God was the guiding idea and chief end of Jesus, every step in his life, including his death, was related to that aim and its realization. When the Kingdom of God takes its due place in theology, the deeds of Christ must be interpreted anew.

Since Jesus revealed the divine worth of life and personality, and since his salvation seeks the restoration and fulfillment of even the least, it follows that the promotion of the Kingdom means the application of these social

[11] *The Social Principles of Jesus*, 142.

principles of Jesus. It means that this requires bearing the cross and exercising faith.

This involves every effort, on the part of the Church, to secure more respect for personality, more reverence for womanhood, more stability for the home, more truthfulness, more love. It involves the redemption of social life from the cramping influences of religious bigotry and from all forms of slavery——in which human beings are treated as mere means to serve the ends of others. It involves learning to bear the burdens of the weak. It involves the redemption of society from political autocracies, and economic oligarchies; the substitution of redemption for vindictive penology; and the abolition of war. It calls on us for the faith of the old prophets, who believed in the salvation of nations.

The Church needs the allegiance of college men and women, who have learned to understand in a measure, the facts and laws of human society. The moral obligation for college communities is thus accentuated. These men and women should make a just return for their special opportunities.

The Kingdom of God is the Christian transfiguration of the entire social order. "The Church is indispensable to the religious education of humanity and to the conservation of religion, but the greatest future awaits religion in the public life of humanity."[13]

[13] *A Theology for the Social Gospel.* 145.

CHAPTER X

CONCLUSION

I

The essence of Doctor Rauschenbusch's contribution to Social Christianity is that religion has not one, but two great functions to perform. In human life there are two great entities—the human soul and the human race—and religion is to save both. The soul is to seek righteousness and eternal life for itself; the race is to seek righteousness and the Kingdom of God for all the world.

Much of Doctor Rauschenbusch's teaching is devoted to a presentation of social Christianity as taught by the Hebrew prophets and to a review of the Saviour's teachings concerning the Kingdom of God.

The fundamental social principles of Jesus referred to in all his major works, either directly or indirectly, are "The Value of Life," "The Solidarity of the Human Family", and the "Obligation of the Strong to Stand up for the Weak."

The application of these principles is to be the remedy for the present social evils. In the attempt to bring about the salvation of society is revealed to us the need of constant self-sacrifice, which adds another fundamental principle to the list, namely, "The Cross as a Social Principle."

If we follow the teachings of Doctor Rauschenbusch according to these principles of Jesus, there will be no race prejudice and his doctrine of equality leaves no room for class differences in the Christian social order. His plan like that of Jesus, was to expand the area of the old social order, extending it to all races and nations. He believed with all his heart that approximate equality is the only basis for Christian morality.

In his discussion on the pursuit of riches, he emphasized strongly the injustice of great accumulation of unearned wealth.

All through his writings he gives graphic pictures of the economic system which contrasts the conditions of Want and Plenty. At the very time when wealth was accumulating with magic rapidity, multitudes were galled into pinching poverty.

Doctor Rauschenbusch says that a complete change must take place. Every manipulator of organized forces, "whether Church leader, or Socialist, or Labor agitator or publicist, or business man who has a vision of the new time and is working toward it, is a new evangelist."[1]

His great idea is to drive the spirit of imperialism out of employer as well as employee. Never for a moment, however, does he aim to antagonize or cause rebellion against honest work. A strike leader no more represents the great body of union men than does the imperialistic employer represent all employers as a class. The law of dependence is the vital principle in life, and Doctor Rauschenbusch knowing this fact, taught that men must think in terms of comradeship. He longed for co-operative organizations which would distribute ownership, control, and benefits to the worthy ones of the working class as well as to the capitalist. He felt that true democracy in the economic life was not only possible, but practicable.

He also looked forward to seeing a general system of public ownership, the control by society of the chief means of production, a satisfactory adjustment of the

[1] Baker, Ray Stannard, A Vision of the New Christianity, *American Magazine*, December, 1917.

present unequal wage-system, the abolition of child-labor, the eradication of the military spirit, and all other irritating phases of the labor question.

He firmly believed that all these perplexing problems are wholly within the scope of Christian teaching and that religious leaders must have a prophecy to deliver regarding them. From this time on there must be a new preaching and teaching—the preaching of repentance from social sins and the need of social salvation.

He believed that civilization in this age is approaching the great crisis of its industrial and economic development.

He also believed that the Great World War was a catastrophic stage in the Kingdom of God and that the war problem submerged all other issues including our social problems. However, he held the opinion that if the World War finally leads to the downfall of Autocracy, and the nations emerge into permanent peace, with equal rights for all, it will have been worth its cost.

That he said very little about the problems of reconstruction and the care of the disabled soldiers after the war, is easily explained when we remember that Doctor Rauschenbusch was called to his home in glory in July, 1918, before the armistice was signed. Like many of his other earnest petitions, the prayer for peace was heard in heaven and the request granted even sooner than he had dared to hope.

The whole aim of his writings was to convict society of its responsibility for social sin, and after the conviction, the next step, was to preach the new evangelism which demands a new birth for society. He sincerely believed that the Church must awaken to the gravity of the widespread discontent with the present conditions or lose its spiritual leadership of the toiling millions.

Love for God and a deep-seated love for all men must

dominate every impulse and energy of life if we are to be true followers of Jesus and co-workers in the advancement of the Kingdom of God.

The characterization of Dr. Rauschenbusch's books as found in the third chapter of this thesis is necessarily very brief and disconnected. In order to catch the broad scope of his vision of the new social order one must personnally study this prophet's great teachings.

A few of the outer and inner facts relating to his life marked plainly the path of his progressive thinking; therefore a brief biography of his life was given in Chapter Two of this thesis, preceding the synopsis of his teachings, as found in his books. This little biography serves to furnish a clearer conception of the influences under which he labored as he performed his tasks in social service, and to impress upon the mind of the reader, the sincerity of his message and the force of his thought.

His judgment deserves attention, not merely by virtue of a wide approval of his books by thinking men and women, but by right of a thorough-going scholarship, a ripe experience in human affairs, and a strong position within the Church itself.

His life of poverty furnished breadth of experience, and a closeness of touch with the struggling masses. His deafness encouraged concentration and reflection. In connection with his affliction, one cannot pay tribute to Doctor Rauschenbusch and his worth, without some word about his wife. She was the chief medium between her husband and those about him. She conserved his strength, saved his time, interpreted with fingers or lips, and established communication between him and his admiring disciples, which would often have been impossible without her. In assembly and class-rooms he was assisted by students.

While he was pastor of the church in New York City, he served a great population of wage-earning men and women, which opportunity gave him a correct insight into the exact conditions of the industrial order. Thus, gradually his aim to save souls grew into the ambition to save society likewise.

"Doctor Rauschenbusch had emphatically a German name, but he certainly glorified it."[3] There could be no "modern Germanism" in his loyal American Christian Nature.

Many of his witty and most brilliant expressions have the tone and the ring of a German scholar; nor is it any wonder that his trend of thinking and his philosophy should sometimes have been influenced by German men of letters, since he received a broad education in European schools of the highest rank.

His mind was so completely absorbed in the thought of his message, that sometimes he seems to pay little attention to his English, nevertheless his style has a rare charm.

Numerous references to European scientists, philosphers, and theologians are made, from whose writings some of his strong quotations are given. Notwithstanding these facts, he was a truly loyal American.

His discussions are masterly, terse, pointed and convincing. While he was a logical thinker, much of his writing resembles in its style, an informal, serious conversation, and like most scholarly composers who write many books, he frequently repeats his ideas and important messages; this makes a concise and satisfactory re-classification of his lessons a laborious task.

He is sometimes extreme in the expression of his favor-

[3]From "Boston Letter", by Charles H. Watson, *Standard*, 17, 1918.

ite ideas, and the trend of his thought is then difficult to follow on account of his apparent indifference to logical arrangement. However, his teachings are forcibly and clearly expressed. His original sayings are so striking, so compact, so intense and so unique that any endeavor to reconstruct these pithy utterances is like attempting to paraphrase the Proverbs of Solomon. Every paragraph contains thought enough for an extensive essay, and many times his sentences furnish good texts for lengthy sermons.

It has been said that the illustrious Professor James wrote Psychology so that it was more interesting than fiction. Exactly in the same way did Doctor Rauschenbusch present Christian Sociology.

The personality of the man himself illuminates every page and words are too empty to describe his unique qualities as he gives us his deepest convictions.

His intellect which was keen and deep with an outlook as lively, sane and kind as it was lofty, was animated with a glowing religious spirit. He was decidedly broad and liberal in his beliefs pertaining to individualistic and conventional religion. By a few prominent critics his ideas are called visionary and his teachings pronounced impractical because he seems to advocate spiritual remedies for economic ailments. Yet, no true prophet has exposed more faithfully than he, the pagan forces that are still triumphant in our modern civilization and his is perhaps the most effective and far-reaching voice heard and heeded on the social question today.

II

A few of the more conservative leaders of the Church criticised severely some of the statements as presented in his *"Theology for the Social Gospel."*

On the contrary, students who are broadly acquainted with his life and thoroughly conversant with all his works have no question in regard to the firm foundation of his teachings which are based squarely upon the utterances and the life of Jesus the Christ, his Lord and his God. Deep-seated love and adoration for his Lord and master Teacher, dominated every impulse and energy of his strenuous life as he ministered unto the great mass of suffering humanity.

Doctor Rauschenbusch himself claimed that he was not a doctrinal Theologian either by professional training or by personal habits of mind. For conservative readers he stated emphatically that the social gospel imports into theology nothing that is new or alien.

It is true, he "lodged a terrific indictment against Churchianity," but he did it without hate or bitterness. In all of his criticisms he was extremely kind, genuinely constructive and grandly positive. He explained that the social gospel seeks to put a democratic spirit which the Church inherited from Jesus and the prophets, once more in control of the institutions.

He preached the social gospel without excluding other theological convictions, but his great concern was not so much about speculative doctrines as about the practical application of the definite principles taught by the Man of Galilee whose vicarious suffering was for the salvation of the community as well as for the individual.

He stressed this important fact, that Jesus Christ, Lord of all, set in motion historical forces of redemption which are to overthrow the Kingdom of Evil.

If the Christian Church is to be Christian it must take up the cross and follow him in deed as well as in spirit.

Growth in grace and the spiritual life must have an ethical outcome. Doctor Rauschenbusch, in his discussion on "Churchianity" even went a step farther. He taught that emotional religion is harmful unless it results in righteousness. Worshipping the ideal must be followed by applying the idea. Else our faith "without works" is dead.

According to his interpretations, the old fundamental theological terms get a new enrichment when we get the real vision of the message of the social gospel.

No one can read his books without feeling the throb of sympathy. The indefinable charm about his writings is due to his candid sincerity, tender love, and unswerving loyalty.

In referring to his own personal life he said that he realized that God hates injustice and he felt that he would be quenching the life of God within himself, if he kept silent in the presence of all the social iniquity of the world around him.

Many times his friends grieved for him pleading that he give up his efforts in behalf of the social gospel and devote himself to "Christian" work. From his hospital bed in Johns Hopkins, Baltimore, during his last illness he dictated a paper in which he stated that his life physically had been a very lonely one, and that he was often beset by the consciousness of antagonism of those who might have co-operated with him.

But throughout all of his bitter disappointments his unswerving devotion to duty and unflagging zeal in behalf of his God and his fellow-men enabled him to be a reflector of Jesus Christ his elder brother and close companion. He confessed that people did not care to hear his message; they would take all he had to say about religion, in the way they had been used to it, but "they did not want any of this 'social stuff' ".[3]

Yet, in spite of his many discouragements, his scientific study of the Bible was undertaken to find a basis for the Christian teaching of a social gospel, which study resulted in the writing of his major works. With calm courage he entered upon great tasks from which others would have shrunk. Though a man of flesh and blood, modest and humble, he was gigantic in his virtues and heroic in his accomplishments.

John Coleman Adams of Hartford, Connecticut, declares, "He was a prophet of the highest type, called and endorsed by God to bear a vital message to his generation."

His deep convictions, kindly sentiment, common sense and indomitable courage enabled him to be a practical idealist.

Some one has said that Walter Rauschenbusch was our "American Savonarola."

"He was one of the biggest men of all the world. Like all who are truly great his real stature was only recognized by the most discerning and he will grow ever larger in the estimate of humanity he so much loved and served."[4]

III

No genuine Christian's power can ever be measured but it is safe to say that the helpful influence of this godly man has circled the globe. His books have been published in many languages. *"Christianity and the Social Crisis"* as well as *"Prayers of the Social Awakening"* have been translated into French. *"Christianizing the Social Order"* has been published in Norwegian and Finnish, while in 1918 arrangements were under way for its transalation into Swedish.[5] Henry Hugo Guy of

[3]The Rochester Theological Seminary Bulletin, *The Record*, November, 1918, P. 52.
[4]*Quay Rozelle*, Philadelphia.
[5]The Rochester Theological Seminary Bulletin, *The Record*, 66.

Berkeley, California, had made arrangements with a Japanese to translate "*Theology for the Social Gospel*" into the Japanese language.

Thomas J. Villers of Detroit, Michigan, said that he knew of no man who was having such power for good on British workmen. The wholesome influence of this friend of every class was the same upon the poor, illiterate laborer as upon the rich and popular scholar.

It is doubtful if any other well known writer on social interpretations is more often cited in collateral assignments by teachers of social Christianity in American colleges and universities than is this modern prophet of a new social order.

His instruction concerning the obligation of every disciple of Jesus Christ is bound to create in man today a more sensitive and a more modern conscience.

How he yearned for big-hearted, big-idead Christian men to get together, to sink their differences for the common good, to make a determined co-operative drive to work out a practicable solution of the colossal problems with which organized society has struggled so fruitlessly these many years! How beautifully by his own consistent life and impersonation of the loving Savior himself, he broadcast to the ends of the earth, the keynote of his deep convictions, namely; that sin ruins, righteousness establishes, and love consolidates!

A person's deepest self is most surely seen in the searching expression of sincere prayer. There, if anywhere, is a man's true heart clearly exposed. Doctor Rauschenbusch in his own book of prayers revealed that calm assurance of his simple faith in the God whose omnipotent love he never questioned. He firmly believed, "If the mysterious will of our souls some how reaches and moves God so that our longings come back from him as a wave of divine assent, which assures their ultimate fulfillment,—then it may mean more than any man knows, to set Christendom praying on our social problems."[6]

This implicit faith and child-like confidence in an all-wise and loving Father, is shown very clearly in the final petition of his *"Prayers of the Social Awakening,"* and with this quotation we conclude our study of *Doctor Rauschenbusch and his Contribution to Social Christianity."*

"O Thou who art the light of my soul,......I know that no word of thine shall return void, however brokenly uttered. If aught in this book was said through lack of knowledge, or through weakness of faith in Thee,.... I pray Thee to over-rule my sin and turn aside its force before it can harm Thy cause.

Pardon the frailty of Thy servant and look upon him, only as he sinks his life in Jesus, his Master and Savior. Amen."[7]

[6] The Rochester Theological Seminary Bulletin, *The Record,* 50.
[7] 'Prayers of the Social Awakening," 126.

SOURCES

Baker, Ray Stannard, Comments on "New Evangelism." *American Magazine*, LXIX, 1817.
Baker, Ray Stannard, "Conversation with Walter Rauschenbusch" in "Spiritual Unrest." *American Magazine*, LXIX, 177-9.
Baker, Ray Stannard, Personality of Walter Rauschenbusch. *American Magazine*, December, 1909, 179.
Rauschenbusch, Walter, Life of. *New International Encyclopedia*, XIX.
Rauschenbusch, Walter, Portrait of. *Review of Reviews*, XLVII, 121.
Rauschenbusch, Walter, Life of, *Rochester Theological Seminary Record*, Rauschenbusch Number, November, 1918.
Rauschenbusch, Walter, Life, *Who's Who in America*, X, 1918-1919
Rauschenbusch, Walter, "Information concerning his life," *Personal letter* from Clarence Barbour, President of the Rochester Theological Seminary, February, 1, 1921.
Taylor, Graham, Appreciation. *Survey*, XL, 493-5.

BIBLIOGRAPHY

I His Books

A Theology for the Social Gospel,
    The Macmillan Company, New York, 1917.
Biography of August Rauschenbusch, n.p., 1901.
Civil Government of United States, n.p., 1902.
Christianity and the Social Crisis,
    The Macmillan Company, New York, 1910.
Christianizing the Social Order, the Macmillan Company,
    New York, 1912.
Life of Jesus, n.p., 1895.
Prayers of the Social Awakening, The Pilgrim Press,
    Boston, 1910.
The Social Principles of Jesus, Association Press, New
    York, 347 Madison Avenue, 1916.

II Lesser Works

Cement of Society, Pilgrim Press, Boston.
Coleman, George W., *American Magazine,* LXXII, 183-5.
Dare We Be Christians, Pilgrim Press, Boston, 1914.
Four Prayers Before Meat, *American Magazine,* LXIX, 289.
Ideals of Social Reformers, *American Journal of Sociology,* II, 202-19.
Influence of Historical Studies on Theology, *American Journal of Theology,* XI, 111-27.
Is the Baby Worth a Dollar? *Ladies Home Journal,* XXVII, 19.
Moral Aspect of the Woman Movement, *Biblical World,* XVII, 195-9.

New Evangelism, *Independent*, LVI, 1056-61.
Prayers for Business Men, *American Magazine*, December 1909, 182.
Prayers for Children Who Work, *American Magazine*, December, 1909, 185.
Prayers for Doctors and Nurses, *American Magazine*, December 1910. LXXI, 1.
Prayers for all Employers, *American Magazine*, LXX, 145.
Prayer for the Idle, *American Magazine*, LXX, 569.
Prayers for all True Lovers, *American Magazine*, LXX, 713.
Prayer for all Mothers, *American Magazine*, LXXI, 145.
Prayer for all Teachers, *American Magazine*, LXX, 433.
Prayer in Time of War, *Independent*, LXXX, 12.
Prayer for Women Who Toil, *Conservation of National Ideas*, Edited by Mrs. D. B. Wells, and others, 100.
Religion of the Passion Play, *Independent*, LXIX, 689-93.
Rights of the Children in the Community, *Religious Education*, X, 219-25.
Section of United States, in *Krüger's Church History*, n.p., 1909.
Stake of the Church in the Social Movement, *American Journal of Sociology*, XXX, 18-20.
The Church and Social Reforms, *Conservation of National Ideas*, Mrs. D. B. Wells and others, 101-22, Fleming H. Revell Co., New York, 1911.
Unto Me, The Pilgrim Press, Boston, 1912, Zurich Anabaptists and T. Münzer, *American Journal of Theology*, IX, 91-106.

www.ingramcontent.com/pod-product-compliance
Lightning Source LLC
Chambersburg PA
CBHW050832160426
43192CB00010B/1994